I0167459

Giants Fall

A Play By

Edward Eaton

Published by
Dragonfly Publishing, Inc.

This is a work of fiction. All characters and events portrayed in this book are fictitious. Any resemblance to real people or real events is purely coincidental. All rights reserved. No part of this book may be reproduced electronically or by any form or by any means, nor may it be rebound, without the prior written consent of the Publisher and the Author. All rights of this play are strictly reserved and applications for permission to perform it, for either professional or amateur productions, must be made in advance to the playwright.

GIANTS FALL

Hardback Edition
EAN 978-1-941278-20-8
ISBN 1-941278-20-5

Paperback Edition
EAN 978-1-941278-21-5
ISBN 1-941278-21-3

eBook Edition
EAN 978-1-941278-22-2
ISBN 1-941278-22-1

Story Text ©2015 Edward Eaton
Cover and Illustrations ©2015 Terri L. Branson
Dragonfly Logo ©2001 Terri L. Branson

Music ©2013 Edward Eaton
Used with permission

Published in the United States of America by
Dragonfly Publishing, Inc.
Website: www.dragonflypubs.com

TABLE OF CONTENTS

Music

About the Author

* * * * *

Dedication

*This work is dedicated to my wife, Silviya,
and to my little man, Christopher.*

Sine quibus non

* * * * *

Dramatis Personae

Trojans

Hecuba: Queen of Troy, de facto ruler now that Hector is slain and Priam has withdrawn. [Female. 50s-70s+]

Paris: Prince of Troy. One of the very few remaining sons of Priam; senior among them. [Male. Mid-late 20s]

Helen: Paris' 'wife'. Also wife to Menelaus, king of Sparta. She is the reason for the war. She is the most beautiful woman in the world. [Female. Early 20s]

Briseis: Paris' cousin, Achilles' slave [Female. 15-20]

Chorus: Trojan Women (1-4) [Female. 20s-30s]

Greeks

Nestor: An ancient king. [Male. Ancient]

Odysseus: A king. [Male. 25-35]

Ajax: Another king. [Male. 25-35]

Achilles: The greatest hero of his age. [Male. 20-25]

Chorus: Greek Soldiers (2-4) [Male. 20s]

Setting

The play takes place late in the Trojan War sometime after the events of *Hector and Achilles* and of Homer's *Iliad.*

The action takes place in the Greek Camp, Achilles' Tent, Ajax's Tent, The Walls of Troy, Paris' Chambers, and the Battlefield before Troy.

The action of the play takes place over the course of one night.

There should be no lags or delays between scenes or between actions in various locations.

SCENE 1

THE GREEK CAMP

Late afternoon

*ODYSSEUS and the
CHORUS OF SOLDIERS
are playing at knucklebones*

*ODYSSEUS wins several
hands in a row*

CHORUS OF SOLDIERS

Damn it! Another
Lucky roll, Odysseus.
He has the gods' luck.

Or does the clever
King help himself to Hermes'
Good fortune. Hush. Hush.

Do not speak so of
Our betters. One more.

Rolls

      Damn it!
I only have a

Few left. One more. Wait,
Lord. Hermes! Bless my roll. Oh,
Tyche, guide my hand!

Now. I feel it. There!
Thank the gods! Odysseus,
Beat that score!

ODYSSEUS rolls

    Damn it!

What meats have you burned?
To what gods have you burned them?
The gods can't back him

Every roll. We
Win sometimes, but the wily
One keeps ahead.

ODYSSEUS
    I
Cheat

CHORUS OF SOLDIERS
    What?

ODYSSEUS
    I cheat.

CHORUS OF SOLDIERS
    Huh?

ODYSSEUS
Are you as deaf as you are
Stupid. I'm cheating.

CHORUS OF SOLDIERS
You're cheating.

ODYSSEUS
    I am.

CHORUS OF SOLDIERS
Wait! You cannot be cheating.

ODYSSEUS
Why not?

CHORUS OF SOLDIERS
Why tell us?

ODYSSEUS
Why not?

CHORUS OF SOLDIERS
What?

ODYSSEUS
Why not?
Does it make a difference?
You suspected it.

CHORUS OF SOLDIERS
I did not, my lord.

ODYSSEUS
You said it just a moment
Ago.

CHORUS OF SOLDIERS
It was so
Long ago. Who knows
What was said by whom?

ODYSSEUS
I heard
You. Look, never mind.
I forgive you.

CHORUS OF SOLDIERS
What?

ODYSSEUS

For your insolence.

CHORUS OF SOLDIERS

But you
Are the one cheating.

ODYSSEUS

So?

CHORUS OF SOLDIERS

Are we allowed
To?

ODYSSEUS

Of course not. If you did
I'd have to kill you.

CHORUS OF SOLDIERS

Oh well, then. That's that.
No, wait, lord. It does not seem
Very fair, to me.

ODYSSEUS

Of course it is not
Fair! That's the point! It's your roll.

CHORUS OF SOLDIERS

You can't win ev'ry

Time.

Rolls

Again? Damn it!

ODYSSEUS

Remember. I am cheating.

CHORUS OF SOLDIERS

I had forgotten.

Why do we still play?

ODYSSEUS

Because you might win. Cheating
Does not guarantee

A win. It merely
Improves the odds.

CHORUS OF SOLDIERS

    It still seems
Unfair.

ODYSSEUS

    Not to me.

Look. Why are we here?

CHORUS OF SOLDIERS

To watch as Achilles kills
Paris.

ODYSSEUS

    Are you sure

Achilles will win?

CHORUS OF SOLDIERS

Of course he will. Paris can't
Win.

ODYSSEUS

That is not fair.

No one goes to war
Expecting a fair fight. We
Go expecting to

Win.

CHORUS OF SOLDIERS

If that's the case,
Why would Troy fight? They cannot
Win.

ODYSSEUS

Can they not?

CHORUS OF SOLDIERS

No.

We have Achilles.
No Trojan can stand 'gainst him
And hope to survive.

ODYSSEUS

And though Achilles
Has bested the best Troy can
Boast of, her walls still

Stand. How?

CHORUS OF SOLDIERS

They were built
By gods, are impregnable.

ODYSSEUS

It hardly seems fair.

CHORUS OF SOLDIERS

It isn't. Bastards!
How can we fight a war 'gainst
A town that can't fall?

ODYSSEUS

How can they wage war
'Gainst a hero who can't fail?

CHORUS OF SOLDIERS

Why do they fight then?

ODYSSEUS

Why do you place coins
Upon the dirt ere I roll?

CHORUS OF SOLDIERS

Perhaps you will lose.

ODYSSEUS

Perhaps Achilles
Will stumble, fall, falter, and
Be vulnerable.

CHORUS OF SOLDIERS

Achilles cannot
Lose.

ODYSSEUS

And Troy's walls can't be breached
By man nor by god.

CHORUS OF SOLDIERS

Then why are we here?

ODYSSEUS

Because.... Let's see. Once there was

A philosopher.

CHORUS OF SOLDIERS

What?

ODYSSEUS

Phi…lo…so…pher.

CHORUS OF SOLDIERS

Another Trojan trick!

ODYSSEUS

What?

CHORUS OF SOLDIERS

The bastards!

ODYSSEUS

No! No!

A philosopher's
A wise man.

CHORUS OF SOLDIERS

Oh?

ODYSSEUS

A crafty
Bastard.

CHORUS OF SOLDIERS

Got it. Go
On.

ODYSSEUS

This phil…this man
Moved to Gela. A safe, a
Peaceful place. There to

While away his days
And nights in contemplation
And native pleasures.

CHORUS OF SOLDIERS

Some native pleasures
Would go over well about
Now. P'rhaps we could sack

Gela.

ODYSSEUS

We are not
Going to sack Gela.

CHORUS OF SOLDIERS

Are
Their walls strong as well?

ODYSSEUS

There are no city
Walls there.

CHORUS OF SOLDIERS

Then they must have great
Heroes to keep off

Enemies.

ODYSSEUS

Heroes
None, nor great armies. Nothing.
There is nothing there.

CHORUS OF SOLDIERS

Nothing?

ODYSSEUS

Nothing.

CHORUS OF SOLDIERS

But
The native pleasures.

ODYSSEUS

What are
You talking about?

CHORUS OF SOLDIERS

The native pleasures.
The reason the…man went there.
For…the native…pleas—

ODYSSEUS

Of course, there are the
Native pleasures and a lot
Of sand. Nothing more.

CHORUS OF SOLDIERS

Nothing? Not even
Houses?

ODYSSEUS

Gods! All right! Houses.
Boats. And fishermen.

And, yes, cattle and
Sheep, and, yes, fish.

CHORUS OF SOLDIERS

What about
Water?

ODYSSEUS

Water?

CHORUS OF SOLDIERS

Yes.

CHORUS OF SOLDIERS

Can't live long without
Water. Is there wine? I can
Live without wine, but

Who would want to?

ODYSSEUS

    Fine!
There's wine. There's everything
One would need to live.

Anyway—

CHORUS OF SOLDIERS

    Then it's
Decided.

ODYSSEUS

    What's decided?

CHORUS OF SOLDIERS

We're off to Gela.

I'll kill fishermen
Any day. What kind of fight
Will they put up? But,

If the fishermen
Have all been slaughtered, who then
Will bring us food? P'rhaps

The women can. When?
During the daytime, of course.
Then what will we do,

During the day? Sleep
Off previous night's revels.
But won't the women

Be tired? Do you care?
They can be asleep for all
I care. Easier.

True. Fish. Three times a
Day. Or four. Or five. If you
Have the stamina.

ODYSSEUS

Shut up.

CHORUS OF SOLDIERS

It's settled.

ODYSSEUS

Shut up.

CHORUS OF SOLDIERS

Pack and we're off to
Gela.

ODYSSEUS

Shut up! We

Are not attacking
Gela.

CHORUS OF SOLDIERS

Then why tease us so
With promises of

Willing women and
Wine, with pleasures to tempt us,
Distractions to ease

The pain, the mem'ries
Of these last years of hardship,
Lives filled with despair?

Odysseus! How
Cruel are you?

ODYSSEUS

Shut up!

CHORUS OF SOLDIERS

To hint
At joy, a heaven

In this horrible
Reality?

ODYSSEUS

Be quiet!

CHORUS OF SOLDIERS

It's so depressing!

Is there no hope left
For us?

ODYSSEUS

The next man who speaks
Dies. Now, where was I?

Gela. There was a
Philosopher....What is it?
What is it? Gods! You

May speak.

CHORUS OF SOLDIERS

You spoke next.

ODYSSEUS

What?

CHORUS OF SOLDIERS

      You
Spoke next. Should you die?

ODYSSEUS

I meant that the next
Person other than me who
Spoke would die. I am

Allowed to speak. Got
It? Got it? You may speak.

CHORUS OF SOLDIERS

      Yes.

ODYSSEUS

Gods give me patience.

Finally. So, this
Philos'pher to Gela moved.
There, while he trod one

Day on the hot sands
In profound contemplation,
An eagle flew by,

A small turtle clutched
In its talons. Mistaking
The philosopher's

Bald pate for a rock,
The eagle dropped the turtle,
Hoping to break the

Shell. Instead, it crushed
The philosopher's skull. So....
Yes? What is it?

CHORUS OF SOLDIERS

Where

Did the eagle come
From? You didn't say there were
Eagles on Gela.

ODYSSEUS

He came from the next
Island.

CHORUS OF SOLDIERS

Why did the eagle
Come to Gela?

ODYSSEUS

For

The turtle. Gods! Look—

CHORUS OF SOLDIERS

And there were no turtles on
The eagle's island?

I find that hard to
Believe. There are turtles all
Over these islands.

ODYSSEUS

All the turtles had
Gone to Gela.

CHORUS OF SOLDIERS

That would be
A lot of turtles

Of course, with all these
Turtles, the women would not
Need to work so hard.

They will not be so
Tired at night. I'm exhausted
Making such effort.

          ODYSSEUS

Shut up! The point is—

        CHORUS OF SOLDIERS

The point is that the eagle
Must have been really

Stupid.

          ODYSSEUS

    Stupid?

        CHORUS OF SOLDIERS

    Yes.
To think that a man was a
Rock. Was it Ajax?

          ODYSSEUS

Hush!

        CHORUS OF SOLDIERS

    Hush!

          ODYSSEUS

    Ajax is
Sensitive. Shh! The point is—

        CHORUS OF SOLDIERS

Maybe it was not

An accident.

          ODYSSEUS

    What?

CHORUS OF SOLDIERS
P'rhaps the eagle wished to kill
The...

ODYSSEUS
Philosopher.

CHORUS OF SOLDIERS
Exactly. Maybe
The eagle sought him out on
A vendetta.

ODYSSEUS
A

Vendetta?

CHORUS OF SOLDIERS
Yes.

ODYSSEUS
You
Know the word 'vendetta' but
Not 'philosopher'?

CHORUS OF SOLDIERS
We are Greek. Vengeance
Is part of our culture, but
Philosophy is

Alien, foreign.
It will never catch on.

ODYSSEUS
Gods.
Anyway, the point

Of the story was

                    CHORUS OF SOLDIERS
Never go to Gela.

                         ODYSSEUS
       Huh?

                    CHORUS OF SOLDIERS
It's a dangerous

Place. Turtles falling
Randomly from the sky to
Kill tourists. Better

Be here.

                         ODYSSEUS
            But there's a
War here. You fools face death on
A daily basis.

                    CHORUS OF SOLDIERS
Exactly. Here, you
Expect arrows and rocks from
On high. You're ready.

It's a war. If you
Are here, you have to know that
Someone, sometime, is

Going to try to
Kill you. It's kind of the point.

                         ODYSSEUS
The story's point is

That anything can
Happen. Accidents can change
Ev'rything.

CHORUS OF SOLDIERS

Unless,

Of course, it was not
An accident. Eagles can
Be very clever.

Ne'er trust the bastards.
Maybe because the man was
Philosopher is

Why he was killed. I
Don't use my brain so much. Hit
Me on the head and

It won't matter much.
I could eat some turtle soup.

ODYSSEUS

Shut up! Gods!

He looks off stage.

Nestor!

*NESTOR enters. He is very
old and very hard of hearing.*

Nestor! King Nestor!
Over here! We're over here!

NESTOR

Well met, young man.

ODYSSEUS

King

Nestor.

NESTOR

Where?

ODYSSEUS

Here.

NESTOR

Who?
Who are you talking to?

ODYSSEUS

You.
You are King Nestor.

NESTOR

Well, that explains a
Lot. King Agamemnon said
To Nestor, "Go and

"Talk to the boys." When
He didn't come back, I came
Looking. That explains

Everything. Yep.
Now I know. Yep. Well, I get
Tired standing all day

Advising great kings.
It would be nice to rest my
Feet a while.

(Beat)

I said:

It would be nice to
Rest my feet a while.

CHORUS OF SOLDIERS

Why don't
You sit by the fire.

NESTOR

Not since last Tuesday,
I think. Do you mind if I
Sit down? I think those

Boys are deaf.

ODYSSEUS

Must be.

NESTOR

Don't you worry. you're still young.
You'll get over it.

I had me a dose
A few years back. Caught it from
A girl from Cairo.

Pretty little thing.
Couldn't piss for months. Well, but
She was worth ev'ry

Drachma, I tell you
What. Ismene. That was her
Name. No. Ismene

Was Oedipus' girl.
Nice girl. Very well brought up.
                                        (Pause)

Had huge tits. Mammoth

Things. Get lost in there.
Don't know how the hell she walked.
Still, she could do things

With her tongue that would
Make Zeus blush. I remember
One time, we were in—

                    ODYSSEUS

What brings you here, sir?

                    NESTOR

Maybe later. What are you
Boys up to?

            CHORUS OF SOLDIERS

        He was

Telling us fables.

                    NESTOR

Hell, give them the damn tables.

Tables in battle?
Kids these days.

                    ODYSSEUS

        What do
You want?

                    NESTOR

        Odysseus. Have
You seen him?

                    ODYSSEUS

        I am

Odysseus.

NESTOR

    Bah!
He's a tall strapping king of
A man. Not a weed

Like you. Where is he,
Ajax?

ODYSSEUS

    I'm not Ajax. I

Am Odysseus.

NESTOR

Are you sure?

ODYSSEUS

    I am.

NESTOR

    Then where's
Ajax?

CHORUS OF SOLDIERS

    He moons o'er

Briseis.

ODYSSEUS

    Or tends
To his sheep.

NESTOR

    I smell nothing.
But, that reminds me.

That reminds me why
I am here. Agamemnon,
High king of all kings

Son of Atreus,
King of Mycenae, king of
Argos, general

And commander of
Our armies, Antiphus' bane—

ODYSSEUS

Get on with it!

NESTOR

    Where?

Duck! Why don't you duck?
Where are they? Don't see them. Don't
See anyone. Bring

Me my sword! Help! Help!

ODYSSEUS

No one's here. No! One! Is! Here!

NESTOR

Thank the gods for that.

Oh! Here is my sword.
Had it with me the whole time.
Well, best to be sure.

Shifty bastards, those
Trojans are. Could be here and
We wouldn't know it.

Saw a young man who
Didn't belong, this morning.
I suspected he

Was a Trojan, so
I had him killed. I asked him,
"Are you a Trojan?"

He said, "No." Can you
Believe it? Just what a spy
Would say. "No." So there

Was nothing for it
But to have his head lopped off.

CHORUS OF SOLDIERS
Was he a Trojan?

NESTOR
Well, no. He was a
Cousin to Diomedes.
Nice chap. Had supper

With him the other
Night. Pity. But, best to be
Safe. Boys, my advice:

Don't trust anyone.
You, boy. Are you a Trojan?

CHORUS OF SOLDIERS
No.

ODYSSEUS
Say, "Yes"! Say, "Yes"!

Before he kills you.

CHORUS OF SOLDIERS
Help!

NESTOR
Trojan bastard.

ODYSSEUS
Say, "Yes"!

CHORUS OF SOLDIERS

Yes! Yes!

NESTOR

Well, good, then.

No Trojan spy would
Ever admit to being
A Trojan. Unless....

ODYSSEUS

He's not a Trojan.

NESTOR

Trojans? Where?

ODYSSEUS

My men are not
Trojans.

NESTOR

Well, then. If

Ajax vouches for
You.

ODYSSEUS

I am Odysseus.

NESTOR

You? Odysseus?

Nonsense. Anyway,
Where was I? I have it. King
Agamemnon, lord

Of Argos—

ODYSSEUS

We heard

That.

NESTOR

You heard that?

CHORUS OF SOLDIERS

We heard that.

NESTOR

Well, if you heard that,

All right then. Let's see....
Lord of.... King of.... Slayer of....
Favored by.... In the

Name of.... here I am.
King Agamemnon begs his
People, the soldiers

Who have risked so much,
Lost so many friends, to know
That the war will soon

End. Agamemnon
Knows, he has heard, that Paris
Will indeed leave Troy

And face Achilles.
With Paris slain, the Spartan
Queen must return, must

Be returned to the
Magnificent—

ODYSSEUS

None of us
Is in his employ.

NESTOR (Sighs)

Once that idiot
Gets his tramp back, we can all
Go home. I'm tired of

These shores. The heat. The
Stench of dead bodies. Ten years!
The adventure here

Has long ago paled.
Our lands have been drained of their
Youths. None left but the

Very old.

ODYSSEUS

So says
Nestor.

NESTOR

The women, and the
Idiots who could

Not be brought to war.
What will be left of our homes?
Ajax? Who rules in

Salamis while you
Dally in Asia?

ODYSSEUS

I am
Odysseus.

NESTOR

Eight,

P'rhaps as late as eight
Thirty. Maybe nine. My lands
Are likely ruined.

My wife died alone
In her bed, her husband leagues,
Many leagues, away,

Stifled in tropic
Heat, or blasted by freezing
Winter winds. How are

Your lands faring? Will
Your wives die alone? Or do
They thrive under some

Other man's caress?
Of course, Ajax. You need not
Worry. Your wife is

Shrewish and she's fat.
Take Odysseus' wife, though.
Penelope could

Hardly wait to get
Him out the door. I hear she
Had a harness built

To keep her legs in
Th'air. Don't tell Odysseus.

ODYSSEUS

I'm Odysseus!

NESTOR

You did? Well, who has
Not at least tried? I did once,
Tell you what. But, hush.

He might be list'ning.
What shambles will we find when,
We return to homes

In disrepair, wives
Unhusbanded and fields left
Fallow? What ruins?

If Paris would just
Step from behind those high walls
And face Achilles.

Helen can be sent
Back. Menelaus' honor—
What's left of it—can

Be satisfied. We
Can abandon these shores, and
Trojans can gather

Their dead and rebuild
Their city.

CHORUS OF SOLDIERS

Can we not sack
This town before which

So many of our
Comrades have lain down their lives,
Sacrificed so much?

NESTOR

How many more of
Your friends will you lose? It was
An ill-conceived war.

ODYSSEUS

Surely, men, you have
Filled your coffers with the spoils
Of an hundred or

More cities that pledged
Allegiance to Troy, as you
Have filled their women.

CHORUS OF SOLDIERS

Somehow our gold drifts
From our coffers and finds its
Way to your pockets.

ODYSSEUS

There's still time, lads. Put
Your coins down and best my roll.
P'rhaps this time you'll win.

NESTOR

Bones! I used to play,
In my youth. Might I try a
Few passes?

ODYSSEUS

    Please do.

CHORUS OF SOLDIERS

Wise Odysseus,
Change your dice. It cannot be
Wise to fleece, er, beat

One so close to the
Great kings. A political
Loss is my advice.

ODYSSEUS

This fool spends little
On wine and less on women.
He can lose a few

Coins. Besides, when he
Whines to King Agamemnon,
He will blame Ajax.

Quickly now. A few
Rolls ere Achilles trods the
Field. An audience

Demands he or, gods
Preserve us, he will come to
Us ere the last act.

They roll and play.

* * * * *

SCENE 2

ACHILLES' TENT

*Late afternoon. ACHILLES
and BRISEIS are in the tent.*

BRISEIS

What if you should die?
What if? Even Paris can
Get lucky. What if?

You're not immortal.
You are not impervious
To sword or arrow.

Yet, the pleas of a
True lover seem not to pierce,
Pull, nor slow you down.

What if you should die?
I do not ask for your soul.
I would not worry.

The shades of victims
Shall part before you when you
First step from Charon's

Ferry and turn your
Sights on Hades' fell domain.
Will you bend your knee

To Death's fell Lord and
Serve Zeus's older brother,
Doing penance for

The many souls you
Sent there ahead of you? Or
Will you rebel, slay

Shadow-clad Hades,
Conquer Hell and bring about
Ever winter by

Seizing sorrowful
Persephone as your prize?
Or do others wait

Your death, your advent
To the Elysian Fields?
Others who will please

You, or torment you.
Far from Briseis' loving
Touch, you will forget.

You will forget this
Child. Me. You will forget my
Touch, my caress, taste.

My Lord, these last months
Have seen me serve as lover,
As mistress, as wife,

As slave to your whims
And passions. I have been what
You desired, needed.

I have been woman.
I have been girl, have been boy,
Even man for you.

Should you die, should you
Fall, by misadventure or
In combat, I will

Be without lord or
Champion. Should you die, what
Will become of me?

My Lord? Achilles?
Lover? Do you feel the lust?
The envy? The hate?

The hate they have? The
Hate men like Odysseus
And his followers

Have for me? Who am
I? Who is Briseis to
Merit the hatred,

The contumely
Of your compatriots, kings
And peasants alike?

Did my wantonness
Drag thousands to perish on
These rocky beaches?

Did I cause this war?
Did I bar great Ilium's
Gates from your envoys?

Did I sit on the
Thrones of great cities in the
Sky, cast down fiery

Arrows and lay waste
To your camps? Did I send plagues
To these perilous

Shores? Pray, Achilles.
Do I deserve the hate? I
Did not seduce great

Agamemnon, nor
Did I abandon greater
Achilles. Not I.

I am but a child.
I should be playing with dolls,
Not being savaged

By ancient kings nor,
Nor serving as doll to a
Robust warrior.

Used. Then to be cast
Aside. A toy, no longer
Fresh, but wearisome.

What will become of
Briseis should Achilles
No longer need her

Or die and cannot
Protect the child any more?
What happens to her?

Do not smirk at me.
I'm not graceful Troilus
Nor brave Patroclus.

I'm but Briseis.
I deserve more than silence.
Consideration

Is my right and your
Obligation. Nor am I
The first to see your

Death in the stars. No.
It takes no knowledge of stars
Nor gifts from lech'rous

Gods to see that you
Will, someday, fall. No. Not die.
Fall. You will surely

Fall. Slain by some dread
Hero. Perhaps an angry
God will defeat you.

Not for Achilles
Quiet old age with hearth and
Home, wives, and children.

You will not die in
Bed. How many great heroes
Live to their dotage?

How many heroes
Have you slain? How many of
Them were the heroes

Of their time? Their lands?
Ev'ry age has heroes and
They must slay, slay the

Other heroes of
The age. In the end, they must
All die. All die. All.

So the next age of
Heroes can rise and take their
Place. Then they will rule,

And in the end, they
Will be slain by new heroes,
Greater and younger.

And then they too must
Fall. Must fall. On and on it
Goes. Heroes rising,

Striving, falling. Your
Legacy awash with blood.
Yours, mixed with that of

Your victims'. Awash
With blood. How long will your soul
Linger to watch those

Living you have left?
Will it appease you when we
Burn incense? When we

Sacrifice to you?
Must we spend our lives mourning
The loss of our great

Heroes? Worshipping
Them? Must you be god in death
As you were in life?

Perhaps some day there
Will be none left to worship
The new heroes. None

Left to weep over
Your remains. None left to fear
For their own small fates.

The gods care not for
The common man. The off'ring
Of a butcher means

Naught to them. What then
The pleas and prayers of a slave?
Will they even hear?

Or worse: will they scoff,
Resent my impudence, and
Punish me that I

Tried? Nor will they hear
Your prayers and save you. Perhaps,
Though, you want to die.

Is that why you strap
On your armor ev'ry day
And wait for Paris

Or whate'er hero
Priam thinks to send to his
Doom and your glory?

Is't not my fate to
Love and die, to rise and fall
Because you seek death?

Is that heroic
Justice? Or is it merely
A quaint Greek custom

That we must honor
As host or as the victim?
Suff'ring in each case?

When you fin'lly die,
Achilles, Lord and Master,
What happens to me?

To what Greek kingling
Will I be sold? To warm his
Bed. To anger wife.

For if I survive
This dread war, I shall no doubt
Not survive the peace.

What wife will welcome
Her husband's pet with naught but
A scowl and a knife

In a shadowy
Stair. Or perhaps sent to men
For whom a slave is

Not delicacy
But beast of burden, less loved
Than the village cow.

So, when you die, Lord
Achilles, Master, Lover,
What's Briseis' fate?

Will you protect me
From the indignities of
Your brutal allies?

Will you defend me
From uxorial fury
Or the hatred and

Envy of peasants?
The lust of soldiers? Tell me!
What will be my fate?

Will they hear your roar
From the Isles of the Blesséd?
Will your bellow sound?

Or simply mew? Or
Be lost ere it crosses the
Acheron on its

Journey to men's ears,
Drowned by cries of your victims
And your dead lovers?

P'rhaps you will linger
By Lethe's smoky shores. There
Forget love and me,

Spend eternity
In a haze of memories
That flit and that dance

Just out of reach, just
Out of hearing, out of sight.
And my cries of pain

And anguish be no
More than an echo of an
Echo of a thought.

Master Achilles,
While you wallow in Hades,
What will be my fate?

Or do you merit
No less than an Olympian
Fate? Great Achilles

Will cast off mortal
Husk and become a god. Will
You overthrow Zeus

And mount his throne? No
Doubt you will mount his wives, too,
And take his sisters.

I may have my charms,
But I pale next to Helen.
What nothing must I

Become when you can
Choose your bedmates from the gods
And the goddesses?

Will you risk Hera's
Rage for me? Or must I face
The ire of Heaven's

Queen simply because
I was, you were, we were? Speak?
What will be my fate?

What will poets say?
They'll sing praises to heroes
Like you and Hector.

They will write epics,
Fill them with tales of battle,
And soak them in blood.

They'll long for queens such
As Helen. Who will sing for
Briseis? No one.

They will scoff at me.
Mock my pain. Care not whether
I lived or I died.

Great Lord Achilles.
What will be my fate? Nothing.
Nothing. Nothing. Naught.

And so Briseis
Sits and suffers the brooding
Silence of her lord.

Here comes one, one king,
Who thinks of Briseis. Would
That I'd been given

To him. To Ajax.
Yes, Lord mine, to King Ajax.
He may be simple,

But he is kindly.
He talks gruff, but means no ill.
And though he takes his

Place before his men,
No heroes seek him, nor Fates
Envy him and try

To cut his life short.
He would not abandon me.
He would not leave me.

See? Here he comes. Stand
Down, great Achilles, for I
Am the object of

This visit. Hail! Hail!
Ajax, son of Telemon.

Ajax enters.

AJAX

Hail! Hail! Briseis.

Lovely lady, hail!

(Nervously)

And of course, my lord, of course.
Hail, Lord Achilles!

BRISEIS

Don't let his scowling
Unnerve you. Come sit. Over
Here. Here. Next to me.

AJAX

That is better.

*He sits on the opposite side of
the tent from BRISEIS.*

                              BRISEIS
            No.
Here.

                                          She motions for him to sit
                                          closer. Eagerly, though
                                          reluctantly, he does.

      Is that flower for me?

                              AJAX
Yes.

                              BRISEIS
            That is sweet.
                          (to Achilles)
            Stop

Scowling. Don't you have
A battle to prepare for?
He gets grumpy.

                              AJAX
            You

Have been crying.

                              BRISEIS
            It
Is the same complaint. He needs
To hear it. You don't.

How are your eyes this
Day?

                                    AJAX
            They get worse when darkness
Falls. It used to be

When I could count the
Men who walked the walls on a
Moonless night. Now I

Can but make out the
Shape of distant Ilium
When the moon is full

And on the rise.

                                    BRISEIS
            There
Are fewer men in Troy, now.
Fewer to walk walls

Or to sortie. P'rhaps
You do not see them because
They're not on the walls.

                                    AJAX

But they are. So I
Can see the light from torches
And hear marching feet.

And Odysseus....

                                    BRISEIS

It's always Odysseus.

                                    AJAX

He is so mean! He's

Snide and mocking!

BRISEIS

Have
You broken with him yet?

AJAX

How
Can I? For there are

Few kings left on these
Shores. Only great commanders
Like Agamemnon

And Menelaus
Who do not speak below them
Save in the voice of

Their messenger, the
Ancient Nestor. And there are
The great heroes like

Achilles. Him and
Epigon Diomedes.
Yet, most of their bones

Lie bleached and crumbling
On the blood-soaked fields of the
Dying city Troy.

Those that do live brood
And wait for glorious deaths—

BRISEIS

From appropriately

Glorious killers.

AJAX

What humiliation comes
To great Achilles?

Your unrivalled lord
Cannot fall to the dreck that
Remains in dulled Troy.

BRISEIS

A city that was
Once my home.

AJAX

   Pardon, lady,
But Priam's seed has

Brought forth many sons,
But few of them of any
Note, and fewer still

Walk under sun's bright
Gaze. Most are ashes that have
Been blown away by

The great gale that our
Armada brought.

BRISEIS

   A deadly
Wind, one that will no

Doubt one day soon gust
And blow poor Briseis down.

AJAX

Say not so, lady.

Let Ajax protect
You.

                              BRISEIS
          How can Ajax protect
When Odysseus

Still numbers among
His friends?

                              AJAX
          Say colleagues, lady,
Not friend. Not friend. No.

P'rhaps I cannot break
With foxy Odysseus.
That is to protect

Myself. The men. They
Listen to his stories. They
Heed his calumnies.

They love whom he loves
And loath the targets of his
Vicious wit. Never

Does he attack those
Above him
                              BRISEIS
          At least not to
Their faces. Many

Times has the wily
Odysseus bent his gaze
Over here and aimed

His wicked tongue at
Achilles

AJAX

In vain does he
Dare aim so high. His

Barbed words cannot reach
Great Achilles, who, as man
As Warrior, is

Impervious to
The attacks of mere mortals.
The great Achilles

Brushes off words from
Odysseus and his ilk,
Ignores their poison,

As he scoffs at the
Arrows and darts of weakling
Trojans like Paris.

The Great Achilles!
The Great Achilles. Does he
Hear? Is he list'ning?

BRISEIS

I do not know. Oft,
He loses self in self, in
Great contemplation.

For hours, perhaps days,
He sits and stares into th'air.
His lips move. No sound.

I know not to whom
He speaks. Does he commune with
The dead? Rail at his

Victims? Call for his
Lovers? Does he see, speak with
Penthesilea?

Or dead Patroclus?
Must he bear the fury and
Scorn of Hector's ghost?

He will not tell me,
Nor can I ask the dead. No
Longer do they crowd

These shores. This war will
Soon end. The Greeks will leave. The
Trojans rebuild their

Once flow'ring city.
Or, better yet, seek out a
Newer, greater place

Not prey to Greece's
Hunger. This war will end. End.
Must. This war must end.

Soon. That is why all
The ghosts have fled. No more to
Condemn us. Never

More to advise us.
They have left us to ourselves.

AJAX

A fate worse than fate—

                    BRISEIS

For we do not know
What fate has in store for us,
But we know hidden

Terrors. We can blame
Gods for our ills. We can blame
But ourselves for fear.

And so Briseis
Sits alone.

                    AJAX

         Briseis sits
With Ajax.

                    BRISEIS

         She does.

And Achilles broods,
Speaks with the invisible.
How are they today?

                    AJAX

How are they?

                    BRISEIS

         Yes. I've
Not seen you for some days. Did
Mwaki-Mu have her

Lamb?

                    AJAX

         A bright gold fleece!
Mother and child are resting.

                    BRISEIS
You must be proud.

                    AJAX
        It's

Psipsino who's proud.
He struts about the flock, as
Cocky as any

Soldier. He chooses
The ewes and bullies the rams.
He stands above his

Fellows with a smug
Look, a superior smirk.

                    BRISEIS

Like many a Greek

I know—peasant or
King

                    AJAX
        Are Trojan warriors all
That different?

                    BRISEIS
        No.

You look like a proud
Father.

                              AJAX
        I feel like one. I
Helped pull the baby

Lamb from the mother
Myself. Only Psipsino
And I are allowed

To approach baby
Or mother. If others try,
Mwaki-Mu bears teeth.

                            BRISEIS
Ewe, tigress, even
She-wolf, all mothers are so,
And all fathers proud.

                              AJAX
P'rhaps ere long, I can
Bring the lamb, a little ram
Like his father, here.

                            BRISEIS
You must! You must!

                            ACHILLES
        Gods!

                              AJAX
Achilles speaks?

                            ACHILLES
        Achilles
Speaks. Do your knees shake?

Does your soul tremble?

AJAX

I…I…I….

ACHILLES

You…you…you…you….
Will you still prattle?

BRISEIS

Achilles roars. Pray
Gods tremble on Olympus
Because you have stirred,

For Briseis shan't.

ACHILLES

Don't push me, woman.

BRISEIS

     Ignore
Him.

AJAX

    He is angry.

BRISEIS

He is bored. He has
Not killed anyone in days.

ACHILLES

Anyone of note.

And Ajax, with his
Tiresome talk about his sheep
Might be worthy of

A blow.

AJAX

    With a sword
I hope.

                    ACHILLES
  Will you quibble?

                    AJAX
    No.

                    BRISEIS
  Leave Ajax alone.

                    ACHILLES
  Don't tell me—

                    BRISEIS
        Stop your
  Bullying. Gods! Ajax comes,
  Sits, and talks with me.

                    ACHILLES
  You are my slave.

                    BRISEIS
          And
  Underused. You can only
  Use your 'mighty blade'

  So many times in
  A day. Even then, you lash
  Out at anyone

  You happen on, man
  Or women, living or dead.

                    ACHILLES
  How was I to know

  Penthesilea
  Was dead?

                         BRISEIS
You had just killed her!

                         ACHILLES
She was mean to me.

                         BRISEIS
She refused to sleep with you.

                         ACHILLES
My point exactly.

Besides, she was quite
Lovely.

                         BRISEIS
        Thanks.

                         AJAX
        I think you are
Lovely, Briseis.

                         BRISEIS
Thank you. That's so sweet.

                         ACHILLES
That's nauseating.

                         BRISEIS
        Shut up.

                         AJAX
More beautiful than

Helen.

ACHILLES

Gods!

BRISEIS

That's sweet.
I know you're lying.

AJAX

That's mean.

BRISEIS

I'm sorry, but she

Is lovely beyond
Words. Thousands of men came here
To fight a war for

Her. Who wages war
For Briseis?

AJAX

I….

ACHILLES
(Overlapping)

I almost
Ended one for you.

AJAX

I….

BRISEIS

Just what a girl
Wants to hear. My epithet:
No one died for her.

                              AJAX
I….

                              BRISEIS
          Not even one
Peasant did you kill for me.

                              AJAX
I….

                              ACHILLES
          I've killed hundreds.

                              BRISEIS
But none were for me.

                              AJAX
I….

                              BRISEIS
          Hector for Patroclus.

                              AJAX
I….

                              ACHILLES
          You made your point.

Penthesilea
For Little Achilles—

                              ACHILLES
          Hey!

                              AJAX
I….

BRISEIS

Sorry! Why did
You kill Troilus?
Why? Why? Oh!

ACHILLES

Hey!

BRISEIS

I won't tell.

Nor would he have. It
Happens to all men. Even
To great Achilles.

AJAX

I....

ACHILLES

I always thought
Agamemnon gave you up
Too easily.

AJAX

I...

I'd start a war for
You!

ACHILLES

Gods!

BRISEIS

That's sweet!

AJAX

I would!

ACHILLES

Gods!

BRISEIS

You don't have to. Please.

But it is nice to
Know you care.

ACHILLES
(Mockingly)

That is so sweet!
Oh, Ajax!

AJAX

Maybe

I should go.

ACHILLES

No. Stay.
I would like to hear about
This war you would fight

For Briseis. Whom
Would you fight?

BRISEIS

My Lord!

ACHILLES

Let me.
Who else would wage war

For Briseis? Would
Illuminated Troy? Would
Priam send his men

To face the might of
Agamemnon's armies? Would
He even send his

Youngest, most worthless
Son to fight you, great Ajax?
Eagle-eyed Ajax?

I'm over here. Troy
Has risked all for Helen, has
Beggared self for her.

Its sons and daughters
Held hostage. Fifty talents
Of gold for Hector's

Body. That is what
They offered me. For a slab
Of meat. Yet not one

Piece of silver nor
E'en copper nor brass do they
Send for Briseis.

There is no hostage
Exchange. Nothing! What little
Do they care for her.

How many men do
You think they would sacrifice
For a used up slave?

Begging your pardon,
'Lady'. Or will you battle
Against your fellows.

You might terrify
The rabble, but high kings like
Agamemnon or

Menalaus would
Scoff at your blustering, and
Vermin, slime, such as

Odysseus would
Not bother with war. No war.
They'd trick you of your

Prize. they'd dupe simple
Ajax. P'rhaps you could best your
Flock of warrior sheep.

AJAX

I...I...I....

ACHILLES

    I..I...

AJAX

I would try!

ACHILLES

    Try?

AJAX

    I'd do my
Best.

ACHILLES

    He'd do his best.

BRISEIS

He would do his best.

ACHILLES

Hector 'tried his best' to kill
Me. Now his ashes

Have been dumped in a
Creek, and his soul floats downstream
In search of a new

Body. King Memnon
Tried his best, as did P'seidon's
Son, Kyenes, and

Even Briseis'
Husband and father. They tried.
They tried their best. Yes.

There is little more
Pitiful than a man who
Tries his best, for he's

Excusing failure
Before he has started. You
Try your best and where

Will Briseis be?

BRISEIS

And so it comes back to that.
What I've been asking.

ACHILLES

She shows no concern
For Achilles.

BRISEIS

   Achilles
Can care for himself.

                              ACHILLES
Achilles will be
Dead.

                              BRISEIS
          You certainly will not
Be alone. You have

Seen to that. I will—

                              ACHILLES
You need not. Ajax.

                                AJAX
          Yes, lord?

                              ACHILLES
Do you want her?

                                AJAX
          Whom?

                              ACHILLES
What?

                                AJAX
          Whom?

                              ACHILLES
          Briseis.
Are you e'en listening? Do
You want Briseis?

                                AJAX
Right now?

                              ACHILLES
          Not. Right. Now.
Gods!

BRISEIS

Easy, my lord.

ACHILLES

After
I'm dead.

AJAX

Oh. Yes, please!

ACHILLES

Fool. Perhaps you may
Keep her long enough to get
Her from this place, this

Camp.

AJAX

My lord?

BRISEIS

My lord?

ACHILLES

I want her safe from the grasps

Of filth like your friend

Odysseus.

AJAX

            I
Will cherish her, honor her.
I will treat her with—

ACHILLES

Shut up! Gods! Look. My
Myrmidons are dead, so give
What little wealth is

Here to distract the
Rabble, then take Briseis
Far away from here.

AJAX

My lord. I will. You
Will not regret this.

ACHILLES

    I do
Already.

AJAX

    I will

Send my wife away
And marry her.

ACHILLES

    Gods! You will
Do no such thing. You

Will send her home.

BRISEIS

    To
Lyrnessus, my lord?

ACHILLES

    Of course
Not to Lyrnessus.

I sacked that town and
Left her people rotting in
The sun. No, to Troy

Or to wherever
Is safe. Can I trust you to
Do that?

AJAX

    I'm your man.

ACHILLES

You're a bumbling oaf.

BRISEIS

My lord, do not tax yourself.

ACHILLES

I do as you asked.

BRISEIS

Yes, Lord. You do as
I asked. You do as I begged.
And I thank you for't.

AJAX

Does Achilles fear—

ACHILLES

He does not. Look, thing. I am
A hero. I can't

Grow old and wallow
On some soft couch to grow gray
And daily watch my

Teeth dull and fall out.
Nor would I want to. What kind
Of life would that be?

To watch your women
Age and wither. To see your
Sons rise and o'ertake

You. Oh, to become
Ancient and decrepit like
Priam. A faded

Life. I pray the Fates
Have not woven that into
My tapestry—an

Endless decay, a
Long, steady, boring life. A
Decomposition

Of my spirit. Gods!
I would rise 'gainst Zeus himself,
Force him to hurl his

Thunderbolt at me
To save precious Olympus
From Achilles' wrath.

If no man can strike
Me down, then I will demand
That the gods do it.

But don't you worry,
Feather-brained Ajax. I don't
Plan to die today.

I will go and stand
Among the rocks and corpses
Before the gates of

Troy and wait in vain,
As always, for Paris to
Come. By midnight, I'll

Be back in my tent,
Scowling, brooding as always.
For now, Ajax—

                    AJAX

My

Lord, I can't begin
To thank—

                    ACHILLES

    No, you can't.

                    AJAX

    If I
Only had the words.

                    ACHILLES

Please do not try.

                    AJAX

    That
You have shown me such a trust.

                    ACHILLES

It's nothing. Really.

                    BRISEIS

Nothing? Really!

                    AJAX

    You've
Taken my hand....You have—

                    ACHILLES

    No.

                    AJAX

Taken my.... Taken...

My hand....

ACHILLES

He has got
To be kidding.

BRISEIS

My lord!

ACHILLES

No!

BRISEIS

My lord. Achilles.

ACHILLES

Oh, very well.

Takes AJAX's hand.

AJAX

You
Have taken my hand!

ACHILLES

And now
Will show you the door.

AJAX

My lord?

ACHILLES

I'm busy.

He goes to BRISEIS.

                                  AJAX

Don't let me keep you. I don't
Mind waiting…Aren't you…?

Oh. Oh! You're busy.
'Busy' busy! Oh my. And
You want me to leave.

                                ACHILLES

In a few minutes,
I will go and stand upon
The wind-swept fields that

Once fed Trojans and
Their allies. There to await
Paris. Will he come

Or yet again hide
Behind Troy's walls? Until then
I would have you gone.

                                                ACHILLES and BRISEIS
                                                go in.

                                  AJAX

So. I'll just wait here.
Then. Go about your. Bus'ness.
I'll just. I'll. Just. Go.

                                                He backs out of the tent.

                              * * * * *

SCENE 3

THE WALLS OF TROY

It is late afternoon.

*CHORUS OF TROJAN
WOMEN is on stage.*

CHORUS OF TROJAN WOMEN

Bitch! Whore! Why does she
Show her face? To torment us?
I don't understand

Why all the men fawn
Over her. And many of
The women as well.

It is disgusting.
Look at her flaunting her clothes
And her jewelry.

Worst, she flaunts her man.
And what a man Paris is?
A stunted runted

Man. No man. All but
A hunchback. Say not so, for
Priam would surely

Have exposed him as
He did so many of his
Sons. Bastards, you mean.

But Paris is no
Bastard. You mean, Hecuba
Bore that toad? I do.

And you saw her push
Him out? Which end did he come
From? Hush! Hush! Really,

He was more feces
Than fetus. Men have died for
Saying less. Priam

Can't afford to kill
Any more men. What men? Where?
Paris is all that

Is left of his brood.
Say Hecuba's, for Priam
Had many bastards.

Most of them are dead.
Paris was exposed. Was he?
Left out in the woods

To be eaten by
Wolves. Or so they say. To die.
He clearly did not.

Die? No. Was raised by
Some rustic. To hear the tale,
Half the farms are home

To bastard children
Of this nobleman or that.
Or, at least, their wives.

Thank the gods my last
Two sons had fair hair. Thank gods
He can't count past nine.

One finger fr'each month.
If they really resembled
My husband, they'd have

Grey hair, creak at the
Knees, and drool. They do drool. They
Drool from their mouths. He

Drools from every
Hole. Ha! But he certainly
Wasn't in Troy at

The last festival
For Poseidon. That was some
Night. It's such a blur.

You did your duty.
I'm such a patriot. You
Are. My husband would

Not understand. He
Would not. My last was a girl.
How nice. Not really.

My father took her
From the nurse and tossed her out.
Tossed her out? Well, not

Literally 'tossed'.
Oh? It was more of a kick.
"Not enough food for

"A girl child. Pop out
Boys, lass." As long as it is
A male, he doesn't

Care who goes in or
Who's comes out. Best not tell him
About the last month's

Services. That was
Nice. Only three more months. Ah!
Do you think…? What? That…

The men…. You know…. Like
We do at the services.
That is different.

What we do is part
Of an ancient religious
Ritual. Our men?

What? Are they Greeks to
Practice such vile…vile…vile what?
Vile atrocities.

What do you think they
Get up to when they are out
Training in the woods

With dozens of men
All waggling their spears at each
Other? My husband

Waggles his spear at
Anything female. Just this
Morning, I found one

Of the slave girls on
His lap. There was nothing for
It but to beat her.

I tried to make him
Watch, but he fell asleep in
The middle. He does

That. How would you know?
Doing my patriotic
Duty. Fair enough.

You don't see Helen
Doing her patriotic
Duty. No. Even

Andromache does.
Not true. She remarried when
Hecuba threatened

To kick her out of
Her suite at the palace. She
Really loved Hector.

And was bride again
Inside a month. Hecuba
Is such a nagging

Slave driver. Where is
Priam? Why does he let this
Crone rule Troy for him?

We need a man's strong
Hand to guide us. Not that aged
Wrinkled old thing. Who's

Hecuba to boss
Us? To order generals?
Who's left to take the

Place of dead Hector
Or mourning Priam? Paris?
Ha! He spends his days

Lolling in bed with
His slut of a wife. They say
That when she's done with

Him, his legs won't work
For an hour. That explains why
Menelaus wants

Her back so. Explains
Why her dresses are so short
In the back and long

In the front. Look at
Her. All dressed up and acting
Like a queen. I'd like

To get my hands on
Her. Me, too. Of course, you would.
Paris is lucky.

No one else is good
Enough for her. So selfish.
She is such a slut!

I know. I wonder
What Spartan diseases she
Has brought here. Ha! Bitch!

Hey, Helen! Yoohoo!
What a lovely dress! See you
Around! What a cow.

Gods. What? Hecuba.
She comes? Until Priam casts
Off mourning, we will

See her ev'rywhere.
How can we fight a war, led
By an old woman?

I can just hear her
Barking orders. Orders or
Not, she barks too much.

They say she was a
Great beauty in her youth. E'en
Great Apollo loved

Her. Troilus was
Their son. So, she fell for that
Old trick, did she? What

Are you saying? "The
God must lie with you. Come to
The temple, drink a

"Holy potion and
Sleep through the exertions of
The divine." What's the

Point then? You would think
The gods would have better things
To do with their time

Than molest mortal
Women, unconscious or no.
What kind of a fool

Would believe nonsense
Such as that? At least after
The second time. And

Certainly after
The third time. Third? Third. Thrice? Thrice.
That's a lustful god.

And a gullible
Husband. Not as gullible
As Io's husband.

When you wake up with
A bull, you have to try. Yes.
Poor husband. Poor bull.

Have you noticed that
After you're with a god, your
Fingers smell like shit?

Yes. But it's divine
Shit. Perhaps, but divine or
No, it is still shit.

Enter HECUBA.

HECUBA

Be gone you crows.

CHORUS OF TROJAN WOMEN

    Caw!
Caw! Caw!

HECUBA

    I'd speak with Paris.
I'd speak with my son.

*CHORUS OF TROJAN
WOMEN exits.*

HECUBA

Paris! Paris! Here!

Enter PARIS.

PARIS

Mother?

HECUBA

    What are you doing?
Why are you still here?

PARIS

Looking for some wine,
Some cheese. I am going to
Watch Achilles storm

About and scream and
Yell. What a fool is he to
Think I would come out.

                              HECUBA

That is the very
Topic about which I need
To speak with you.

                              PARIS

        Ah.

Should I stand before
The gates and taunt the hero
And flee back inside?

What a laugh that is,
But the last time you held the
Gates so long I could

Feel the heat of his
Fury on my neck. Flecks of
Semi-divine spit

Burned into my flesh.
I knew fear, mother.

                              HECUBA

        For a
Hero, fear is naught.

                              PARIS
                            (Sneering)

"For a hero, fear
Is naught." What nonsense, mother.

HECUBA

It is not nonsense.

Did Hector fear to
Face dread Achilles? E'en though
He faced certain death?

PARIS

What is the point, then?
Why fight unless you have a
Chance for victory?

Hector may have been
Brave, but he was fool. He could
Have stayed and embraced

His wife's instead of
Achilles' blade.

HECUBA

   A prince's
Place is on the field

Of battle, not in
Bed, wallowing with women.

PARIS

I am a lover.

I've mastered diff'rent
Skills, stratagems, a diff'rent
Kind of swordplay.

HECUBA

Ha!

It's high time you sheathed
That sword of yours, boy.

PARIS

I sheath
It regularly.

And in a well-oiled
Scabbard.

HECUBA

Your mighty blade has
Done more harm and killed

More men than even
Achilles, Diomedes
Together. Helen

May moan. Your prowess,
Though, makes other women, wives
And mothers, weep. I

Say 't'is time you put
Away your sword and stand up
And be a man.

PARIS

To

Face Achilles? How
Is that brave? Where's the glory
In certain defeat?

Let Paris be. Let
Paris be Paris and make
Love to lovely wife.

HECUBA

While you hump *his* wife
In your chambers, my people
Die. Their blood, their flesh

Fertilizes our
Fields. The water we drink, the
Food we eat, tainted

By deaths. Deaths brought to
Our city because you can't
Aim your deadly thrust.

PARIS

I did not Hector
Send to face Achilles. I
Did not ask Priam

To close the gates of
This fair city 'gainst the hordes
Of filthy Greeks. No.

HECUBA

Yet Hector did face
Achilles. Priam did close
The gates. Our women

Do mourn the loss of
Husbands, lovers, brothers, sons.
They've borne this for you.

They've suffered for you.
Who are you to deserve this?
Who are you not to

Care?

PARIS

     I am Paris!
Who am I? I am your son.
Have you forgotten?

Can you remember
Your child? Your baby? Taken
From your arms. Taken,

To be tossed away
In the woods? Fodder for wolves?
What was I? Garbage?

Did I not look like
Priam? Did I resemble
A god or smell like

The gardener, as
So many of the brood that
Clawed out from 'tween your

Legs? Yet they were raised
In the palace. I was found,
Wrapped in royal sheets,

My skin already
Blue, and my cries feeble and
Weak. Did I ask 'bout

Duty as I gasped
And wheezed, fighting for a breath
Of winter air? Did,

Did you cry out to
The gods to warm me? Did you
Embrace me to calm

My cries? Why were my
Brothers and sisters fated
To grow up knowing

Mother, father, and
I to know hardship, hunger,
Abuse, and worse: to

Know that the mother
And father who should have loved
Me, warmed me, covered

Me with affection
Had me taken to the woods,
To the snow, the cold,

Animals. To die.
You ask if I care. Care for
Priam, Hecuba?

Care for Troy, for my
People? I care as much as....
As much as you cared

For the carcass of
Your infant son. That, mother,
Is how much I care.

HECUBA

I've buried children.
I've watched their bodies lying
In holes, covered by

Dirt and rock. I saw
My baby taken from my
Arms to be left to

Die in winter cold.
I've watched these past ten years as
Brutes no better than

Animals have killed,
Have slaughtered my sons, and have
Raped my daughters. Mine!

Do not claim to have
A monopoly on pain.
I still lie at night,

Images of you
As a swaddled babe, alone
In the night, savaged

By some foul beast, your
Tiny throat torn, flesh devoured
Jolt me awake. O!

They fill me with fear
And terror. But the sight of
So many of my

Sons' corpses, remains
Of my daughters' ravaged souls
Sometimes makes me wish

That when you were just
A newborn babe, I myself
Had bashed in your brains.

PARIS

Mother!

HECUBA

    I suppose
You refuse to fight.

PARIS

    I do.
I shall not fight him.

HECUBA

And there is nothing
I can do to change your mind,
Is there?

PARIS

    There is not.

HECUBA

Well, then. Let us sit
Upon these walls and worry
Not about this war—

This war that has chased
Us from our fields and our ports
And razed the cities

Of our allies—let
Us sit here and remember
Gentler, kinder, days.

PARIS

Days when I looked up
At these walls and longed to go
One day inside them,

Not knowing they were
My birthright.

HECUBA

    Gods! I've heard this
Story many times!

Come, Paris. Drink this.

                    PARIS
It looks like water. And smells.
Not. Like. Wine.

                    HECUBA
        It is

A wine from away.
Even though we are at war,
We must send out our

Merchants to make new
Friends. Drink up!

                    PARIS
        What care I for
Merchants' friends. I am

A prince.

                    HECUBA
        Do you have
Any idea how an
Empire works, young prince?

You men, you soldiers,
Bluster and rage and kill each
Other. Merchants are

Signing treaties and
Building trade. Commerce. Commerce,
Boy. That is whence our

Wealth and power come.
Don't get me wrong. War empires
Spreads; Commerce keeps them.

Drink more. Liquor found
In the marshy lands west of
The great forests and

By the churning seas.
Made from juniper berries.
The children there, they

Say, drink this as if
Mother's milk? More? Fine. We've much.
They're out there, you know.

                    PARIS

Who, mother? Crikey!

                    HECUBA

Too rough?

                    PARIS
          Smooth. Smooth. Give me more.

                    HECUBA

If it is too strong....

                    PARIS

Nonsense, mother. Should
A Trojan prince be bested
By barbarian brats.

                    HECUBA

I'm just a woman.
Anyway, they are laughing.
We know. We have spies.

                    PARIS

Laughing? At us? The
Bastards!

HECUBA

No matter.

PARIS

To laugh
At us...To mock us....

How dare they? Kill us—
Fine. Destroy our culture, our
People—be that as

It may. But they must
Respect us.

HECUBA

I agree. The
Songs they sing of us.

How Hector soiled self
On the field of battle when
He faced Achilles.

PARIS

Infamy! Where is
That flask? Oh!

HECUBA

The things they say
Of you.

PARIS

What say they?

HECUBA

They call you: 'Paris...
The lesser.'

                              PARIS

'Paris'? 'Lesser'?
Those…. Those….

                              HECUBA

        Those?

                              PARIS

        Yahoos!

'Paris the lesser,'
My ass.

                              HECUBA

        They say *that* about
You as well.

                              PARIS

        As they

Are Greeks, it's hardly
An insult for them.

                              HECUBA

        I guess
Not.

                              PARIS

        Disgusting as

It may be. Stupid
Greeks.

                              HECUBA

        Up the palace, women
Drink that with water,

Slightly warmed. Would you
Like some water?

PARIS

Ha! Drink like
Women? Give me more!

HECUBA

That's exactly what
They call you.

PARIS

Me? A woman?
Damn those filthy Greeks!

To slander me? Me?
I who have stolen their most
Precious of treasures.

I have taken her.
I have taken Helen. He,
Menelaus, could

Not keep her. I could.

HECUBA

They maintain that she keeps you.

PARIS

Dare they say so?

HECUBA

Yes.

PARIS drinks.

There is plenty more.
It is like water to them.
To them, like water.

PARIS

Weaker than water.
Keeps me? Bastards! Who do they...?
Who they do? Do? Who?

HECUBA

'Who do they think they
Are?'?

PARIS

    Exactly, dear mother.
Those filthy vile Greeks.

Need I say 'filthy'?
Need I say 'vile'? 'Loathsome'? What
Word is worse than 'Greek'?

Bring me.... Bring me...him.

HECUBA

Menelaus?

PARIS

    Him, too! Bring
Me Menelaus!

HECUBA

They say, the Greeks do,
That Helen mounts you.

PARIS

    Mounts me?
That *Helen* mounts *me*?

HECUBA

Yet Menelaus
Rode her stallion-like into
The Spartan dust.

PARIS

O!

HECUBA

If Helen rides you,
Menelaus rides her, then
The Spartan rides you.

PARIS

Villainy! Spartan
Lies! Greek cunning! Infamy!
Dare Menelaus

To speak so to my
Face? No Trojan should suffer
Such indignities!

Villainy! My sword
Waits to succor the bloodied
Pride of wife and kind.

My arrow will be
True and deadly as Zeus' bolt.
I'll leave the field strewn

With their carcasses.
Damn them! Damn them to Hades
To say so of me!

HECUBA

And Achilles says
That ere this war ends, he'll use
Helen's mouth to sheath

Both his mighty blades.

PARIS

He didn't!

HECUBA

He didn't say
Which blade he'd use first.

                    PARIS

O! That I should live
To hear such things said about
My angel. My Love.

That scum. That brooding
Prince. He's not that dangerous.
I can defeat him.

I'm faster than him.
Cleverer. Hector failed 'cause
He tried to beat strength

With strength. I have speed.
I have more cunning than e'en
Great Odysseus.

I know these pastures
Better than any soldier.
I was raised on them.

You're dead, Achilles!
D'you hear me? You're dead! Dead! Dead!
You watch, mother. Watch.

                                        HECUBA offers him some
                                        more liquor.

Nope. Do not need more.
Going to kill Achilles.

                    HECUBA

There's a chill tonight.

                    PARIS

It is a bit brisk.

HECUBA

Perhaps one flask.

PARIS

Make it two.
I'll show those bastards.

He leaves.

HECUBA

Paris! Boy! The gate
Is that way.

PARIS reenters.

PARIS

The gate is that
Way.

He leaves in the other direction.

HECUBA

Find some weapons!

PARIS (Off)

Yes, mother!

HECUBA

Gods help
Troy that her people rely
On his feeble wits.

* * * * *

SCENE 4

THE GREEK CAMP
THE TROJAN WALL
ACHILLES' TENT
THE BATTLEFIELD

> *ODYSSEUS, AJAX, and*
> *NESTOR, and* CHORUS
> OF SOLDIERS *are in the*
> *camp.*

ODYSSEUS

Achilles wants to
Give you lovely Briseis?
Congratulations

AJAX

He wants me to take
Her back to her home, to Troy

ODYSSEUS

That is nonsense.

AJAX

Why?

Say you so?

ODYSSEUS

If he
Wanted Briseis returned
To hearth and to kin

He would simply send
Her back. Great Achilles wants
You to have her. Ha!

Wants you to take her.

                    AJAX

He said to take her home.

                    ODYSSEUS

        He
Wants peace and quiet.

You know she rules in
His tent. He rarely beats her.

                    AJAX

That is true.

                    ODYSSEUS

        She ne'er

Screams in pain, though in
Anger sometimes cries. Or are
They screams of passion?

Does she speak much? Pray,
Tell me what she says. Ignore
These fools. Is it true

That Trojan royal
Sluts pluck all their hair and smooth
Themselves with bees' wax

And pumice?

                    AJAX

        I...I....

ODYSSEUS

Have been so closed mouthed about
Achilles' tent.

AJAX

There's

Really nothing to
Say.

ODYSSEUS

You're no fun.

AJAX

Say not so!
They've given me trust.

Achilles has ta'en
Me into his tent. He…he.
Has. Shaken. My. Hand.

ODYSSEUS

And why would you be
So singled out?

AJAX

Achilles,
And Briseis, one

Day watched me battle.
I saw the divinely born
Aeneas across

The field of conflict.
I bellowed forth my challenge
Then stalked the hero.

Back and forth we went,
Fighting, seeking each other.
Two mighty kings in

Mighty combat. P'rhaps
The poets will sing of our
Confrontation. P'rhaps.

P'rhaps not, for I lost
Aeneas in battle's gloom
And confusion. As

I sought my foe in
Increased desperation, I
Trod, distracted, in

The shallows of Troy
Loving Simois. So, did
The god spy me from

His perch on the peak
Of Mount Ida. He flew down
And there did pull me

Under his raging
Current. There we fought out of
Sight of mere mortals.

I raged against him,
Dealing him many wounds he
Will not soon forget.

Though I am master
Of arms and feared by many
Men—Trojan and Greek—

I am no match for
The gods. So, Simois dragged
Me under and would

Have taken my breath,
My life, had not Achilles
Come to my rescue.

He chased the angry
God from the field and carried
Me back to his tent,

Risking the fury
Of the gods—Olympian
Wrath—as he saved me.

On my return to
The mortal realm from places
So terrifying

My mind fears recall
Them, I learned that Briseis
Had bad Achilles

Dare divine fury
For my worthless hide. I know
Not why he did as

She begged, but he did.
I survived the attack, and
For that I thank him.

ODYSSEUS

Let me get this right.
One afternoon, you thought you
Saw someone across,

Way across, the plain.
You went over there and found
No one. You sat on

A rock and drank some
Wine to clear the dust from your
Parched throat. You drank too

Much wine, as you do,
And fell into the river.
Drunk, fat, weighed down by

Armor and trophies,
You could not rise until you
Were lifted by him,

By Achilles.
                              AJAX
        We…
We were almost slain on our
Return by wrathful

Gods.

                         ODYSSEUS
        On you way back
It started to rain. That right?
And there was thunder.

                           AJAX
You don't understand.

                         ODYSSEUS
Ajax, you're an idiot.
Friend, but idiot.

Stop moaning over
Briseis. Achilles will
Not die soon. We had

A new girl sent down
The other day for us to
Keep for a week and

Then send down to the
Men. A girl with black silken
Hair who comes from the

Land, they say, whence comes
The sun. Exotic. Willing.
Leave off Briseis.

Her kind is for Great
Kings and heroes. Be content
With what you're given.

Once those gates open,
There'll be gold and pleasures for
All. Until then, be

Patient. Don't cast your
Sights, your desires, above your
Station. Our station.

Do you merit more
Than me? Better prizes? More
Honors? I'm your friend.

Understand I'm right.

AJAX

Great Achilles warned me of
You, Odysseus.

He said that he would
Gift her to me, unless you
Tricked me of my prize.

ODYSSEUS

Did he? If goddess
Spewed Achilles truly wants
To give you his prize,

Then my cunning, such
As it is, cannot take her.
Trust me on that, friend.

AJAX

I am sorry that
I doubted you. You're my friend.

ODYSSEUS

Let's watch the battle.

NESTOR

This will take a while.

CHORUS OF SOLDIERS

You think he will fight today?

NESTOR

You can count on it.

CHORUS OF SOLDIERS

What do you know, old
Man?

NESTOR

So many things.

CHORUS OF SOLDIERS

    To storm
This city. That would

Warrant the many
Years of war we have spent here.

NESTOR

This is not war!

CHORUS OF SOLDIERS

    Not?

NESTOR

No, boys. Here we sit.
For ten years. On the beach. Dare
You call this war? You

Think it glorious?
How often do we sortie?
Ha! From time to time,

Some brat who claims to
Have divine blood steps out and
Roars and challenges

Some other divine
Bastard. P'rhaps I should challenge
Priam. We are of

And age. Ha! So, here
We sit, in the muck, and pray
To die in battle

Ere the plague kills us.

CHORUS OF SOLDIERS

A plague divinely sent to
Punish us. If the

Gods will it, mortal
Man cannot escape death. Nor
Should we dare try to.

T'would be impious
To try. We should pray that they
Forgive us our sins.

NESTOR

Stuff and nonsense. The
Gods send no plagues to punish
Us. The gods must be

More efficient than
That.

CHORUS OF SOLDIERS
What mean you?

NESTOR

If P'seidon,
Mighty Poseidon—

CHORUS OF SOLDIERS
Who favors Troy!

NESTOR

Good
For them. If the god wanted
Us dead, why not send

A great wave to wash
Us 'way?

CHORUS OF SOLDIERS
A wave? Where? Quick! Hide!

NESTOR

You can't hide from a

Tidal wave. Find high
High ground.

CHORUS OF SOLDIERS

Troy is on a hill.
P'rhaps we could hide there.

Would they let us in?
Perhaps if we asked nicely.
All right. Let's go!

NESTOR

Stop!

There is no great wave.

CHORUS OF SOLDIERS

No?

NESTOR

No!

CHORUS OF SOLDIERS

Then why scare us so?

NESTOR

I'm simply saying

That if the gods wished
To kill you, they could send a
Wave to wash away

This camp, the ships, and
The armies and cleanse this shore.

CHORUS OF SOLDIERS

A wave would be a

Wasted effort, for
The gods have already sent
A plague to kill us.

NESTOR

The gods did not send
This plague.

CHORUS OF SOLDIERS

There is plague, so the
Gods must have sent it.

NESTOR

What do the gods have
To do with it? You men have
Lived these past ten years

In a ditch, dug in
Wet ground, that you share with your
Waste and your garbage.

The air is filled with
The rotting stench from corpses
Of both friend and foe.

Our fresh water is
So filled with waste and ashes
Of the dead that you

Could make bricks with it.
There's no wonder there is plague.
There's wonder we live.

This is no way to
Fight a war. They hide in their
Fair city, watching

As their lights dim, as
Their civilization fails,
As their overlords,

Their allies, their friends
Abandon them to their fates.
And we huddle in

This disease-ridden
Camp and watch our men rot, die.
Is no kind of war.

Some years ago, we
Went to a far off land—far,
Far to the west. Far.

There, the people were
Black as night and fought naked
As the day you were

Born. Their cities great
Adobe kraals. Their women?
They lived, worked, and played

Half naked. I can
Still see their huge tits bouncing
As they walked. Up. Down.

Up. Down. Up and down!
They were so firm! Those women
Would simply rut right

In the middle of
The damn street. Insatiable,
They were. Never did

Learn their language. Who
Wants to talk to the foolish
Women. Just want to

Hear them grunt. 'Grunt!' 'Grunt!'
They'd go at it like farm beasts,
From morning 'til night.

Our men could barely
Walk by the end of the day.
They should've sent the

Women first. Their men
Could have killed us after the
Sex and we would have

Thanked them for the rest.
As it was, the men were dead.
Gone. There was nothing

For it but to gut
The savage bitches before
We left. Merciful.

'Twas merciful. I
Thought it might be nice to take
Home some Trojan slut.

Not as voracious
As the black ones were, but the
Cooler winters won't

Kill them. But it looks
Like that will not happen now.

CHORUS OF SOLDIERS
What does that mean, lord?

NESTOR
What does what mean?

CHORUS OF SOLDIERS

    Are
We not meant fair Troy to sack?
Prisoners to take?

NESTOR

O'er there by the boats,
I'm sure. Me? I want to watch
The fight.

CHORUS OF SOLDIERS

    What are you

Talking about?

NESTOR

    Just
Afternoon, I thought. Quiet!
Was that Achilles?

                          BRISEIS in ACHILLES'
                          TENT.

BRISEIS

How empty it is.
How empty the tent of my
Master. Once it was

Full of men, full of
The sounds of soldiers as they
Prepared for battle.

Once it was full of
The groans of wounded. Those who
Fought 'gainst a worthy

Foe and died s'rounded
By comrades. Once it was full
Of the cries of the

Women taken by
My master and his minions.
Tears, pleas, filled this place.

Once it was full of
The ghosts of the fallen, ghosts
Of friends and foes who

Made obeisance to
Achilles ere they made their
Journeys to Hades.

Now it is shared by
Me and my master, lover.
And I am alone.

He stalks the field in
Search of a worthy death though
All his peers are dead.

So, I am alone.
Do I want my lord to die?
Then I can return.

Return to Troy. Home.
Return to what? My husband?
Slain. Achilles took

Me that first time still
Dripping with his blood, his and
That of father and

Brothers. It was still
Warm upon his hands and lips.
Return to mother?

I could hear her cries
As the men passed her from one
To another at

That moment when my
Lord spilled his seed inside me.
My cries of shame and

Hers mingled for a
Moment. They danced in discord
With the jeers and grunts

Of the men who took
Us. They took her, my mother,
To be used and then

Cast out. Alive, dead
No matter to the Greeks. Though
Better dead, for there'd

Be nor life nor hope
Nor beauty left after they
Were done with their games.

I, to be ta'en, raised
Above other slaves, above
Men and kings, above

E'en glory. Far more
Pampered am I in chains than
I e'er was in furs.

I dine better than
Emperors. My wine is fresh,
Unwatered. I am

Kept by the Hero,
Not passed around by peasants
Or sold to allies.

I am freer as
Slave than so many who live
Freely in besieged

Troy. Do I want to
Return to Troy. To playmates?
What has been their fate?

Do their husbands live?
Do their children abuse them?
Are they hungry? Or

Is it their cries I
Hear as I lie next to my
Hero? When I was

A child, I would dream,
Dream, dream of being taken
By a man straight out

Of legend. Now, now.
I have my dream now. I have.
My dream. My hero.

Do they mourn for me.
Or do my childhood playmates
Envy me my fate?

Do they long for my
Hero's embrace? More like, they
Loath Briseis for't.

Do I want to stay?
Pray doomed lover lives. Pray Greeks
Let me leave empty

Tent and return to
Dying city, or let me
Cast myself upon

His pyre so that the
Fire can savage me, or else
The Greeks surely will.

How empty it is.
Empty is the tent of my
Lover. Once it was

Full of life. Full of
Sound. Now it is quiet. Now.
Now, it waits for death.

                                                PARIS is on the battlefield.

                              PARIS

"The wrath of Paris
I sing, who sallied forth from
The walls of Troy to

Face fell Achilles.
And the woman who loved him."
That doesn't sound right.

Hmm. Let's see. "I sing
The arms of the gracious prince."
Ha! Song about arms!

What foolishness! "Hear!
We've heard of Trojan heroes
And the glory…." Hell.

What will the poets
Sing of me? Am I hero
Of this epic tale?

Or am I villain?
Am I a lover? Or am
I the whoremaster?

In my heart I am
Lover. Perhaps not hero.
Certainly victim.

Victim to gods' whims.
Victim to ministrations
From this era's most

Beautiful woman.
Whenever. Whatever. I.
Want. Whomever. I

Want. In one woman.
Infinite variety
Of technique. Approach.

Even appearance.
Helen is everything
Any man could want,

Could desire. E'en change.
The most succulent meats, the
Sweetest wines, the most

Profound music, e'en
The loveliest girls pale and
Diminish when they're

Overused and there's
No variety. But with
Helen, ev'ryday

Is a visual
Sexual adventure. Gods!
There's she on the wall.

Ready. Waiting. P'rhaps
I should go back and take my
Quaint wife and fight some

Other day. Perhaps.
Will he wait? Will Achilles
Still stand before these

Gates and dare Paris?
Bellow, and rage? Perhaps if
I stay inside, he

Will tire and go home,
Leave my people to die old,
Me to be king and

Lover. Lover. King
Paris, who took the woman
Of his age. Took her

From a great king and
Who kept her from a vast host
Of fell savages.

Paris. Home then. To
Bed, but not to sleep. Trade big
Death for little death.

Good. Home. Oh, mother.
On the wall next to Helen.
Lover and mother.

Mother and lover.
It cools, no, slays the ardor.
Wave to mother! Hi!

She cannot hear me.
That is good. I am out here.
On my own. To face.

The greatest. Hero.
Of the age. Great Achilles.
Achilles. "I sing

Of Paris, fool and
Idiot and corpse!" There's some
Tale for the telling.

Nor tragedy nor
Epic. A low, base-born farce.
A corpse for hero.

That is not my tale.
That must not me my story.
Must not be my fate.

Let's sit. Consider.
Bow. Flask. Sword. Three objects of
Equal importance.

I've only two hands.
Where's a philosopher to
Help figure the math?

Flask. Sword. Bow. Mother!
She's too far away. I'll have
To do this alone.

Sword. Bow. Flask. What kind
Of hero would leave his sword?
Yet Achilles is

Master of the blade.
I cannot win against him.
Bow? Many Greeks have

Fallen to my fell
Arrows, but will Achilles
Fall prey to them? I

Pray he will. I fear
He won't. Perhaps the gods might
Guide my arrows, but

Why would they? They have
Backed Achilles' moves for so
Long. Flask? I cannot

Lay down the liquor,
For Paris is no fool and
Knows that his courage

Is of the liquid
Kind. Bow. Flask. Sword. One must wait
Behind these rocks. Flask?

Bow? Sword? Mother! Wife!
Cannot hear nor interfere.
Paris is alone.

CHORUS OF TROJAN
WOMEN is on the wall.

CHORUS OF TROJAN WOMEN
Paris looks all right.
A little thin, but all right.
All a little thin.

They're all a little
Familiar. Ten years we've been
Stuck in this city.

Stranded here on this
Island in the midst of war.
What a waste of youth.

I'll be twenty next
Month. You still have a few good
Years left. Could have a

Couple more children.
More? No more! Six was enough.
I suppose. I was

But a child when this
War began. Will I survive.
See my daughter wed,

Be a grandmother
Ere it ends? I can't recall
The flowering fields

Or fat cattle out
To pasture. There are gentle
Streams in those mountains

Did I once splash my
Feet in the cold water or
Bathe in sacred pools?

If so, 'tis only
In dreams, or mem'ries of dreams,
Or dreams of mem'ries,

Dreams of mem'ries' dreams.
Is it true that not all snow
Is tinged with red and

The sea breezes have
Not e'er reeked of Greek waste, dead.
'Tis said. Don't recall.

I do remember
That I met my husband fresh
From a morning's fray.

I took him to my
Bed with stitches sewn by me
Thread cut by my teeth.

Within a month, I'd
Donned a widow's veil. I can
Still see his body,

Flush with youth, with his
Guts pouring through his fingers.
He wept as he died.

He did. Then I was
Wed to a 'great captain' from
The East. Older than

My father he was.
He brought twenty brave men with
Him. Arthritic men.

They were dead in six
Months, though he hobbles on, my
Husband. Hobbles on,

Hobbles home. I was
Wed, widowed, sold, and pregnant
Ere I was thirteen.

Do you think they'll find
A new husband for Helen?
When Paris is dead?

Not before he's dead.
Of course, not before he's dead.
Perhaps Priam will

Take Helen to wife.
Hecuba could use the rest.
I'd not put it past

That old goat. I'd hate
To live in that dim harem.
Have you been? Yes. Once.

It was like being
Made love to by rotting dust.
That sounds unpleasant.

It was. P'rhaps Paris
Will win. Ha! Don't laugh. He could.
What is he doing?

He's sitting on a
Rock, drinking. That's no way to
Defeat Achilles.

Maybe it's a new
Strategy. Men certainly
Fight wars strangely. Yes.

Do you think she'll leave?
Helen? No, Hecuba! Why
Would Hecuba leave?

I meant Helen! Gods!
Have you seen Menelaus?
Bow leggéd. No neck.

And hairy. Like a
Gorilla! I hear the Greek
Women are almost

As hairy as the
Men. Paris had to have her
Plucked like a chicken

And now, she'll be plucked
By another husband. Such
Is a widow's fate.

HECUBA and HELEN
are on the wall.

HELEN

Black becomes me not.
I was made for bright colors
And for gay outfits.

HECUBA

Don't fret so. We do
What has to be done.

HELEN

           Was it
Really the best plan?

HECUBA

You would not go, and
He would not give you up. What
Else could I think of?

HELEN

In your room, it all
Made sense. The Plan. The outcome.
Now, as I watch him....

HECUBA

Stand firm. Be strong. Oh,
You are shivering. Your dress
Is too thin, shoulders

Bare.

HELEN

           Paris likes this
Dress. I wore it for him. I
Sought him out ere he....

HECUBA

I did not want him
To see you. Your farewells would
Take too much time. That

Grecian oaf would not
Wait.

                              HELEN
        So I will leave ere long.
I must leave ere long.

                              HECUBA
After a few days.
If Menelaus will have
You back.

                              HELEN
        He will.

                              HECUBA
        Are

You sure?

                              HELEN
        Yes, I am.

                              HECUBA
Yes, you are. You still shake. Cold
Or nerves. Let me keep

You warm.

                              HELEN
        Your hands are
Strong.

                              HECUBA
        While men posture and fight,
Women do the work.

                              HELEN
And work hard you do,
Mother.

HECUBA

We don't have to wait
Here. Inside is warm.

HELEN

That would be nice. What
Is he doing?

HECUBA

Who?

HELEN

Paris.

HECUBA

Who?

HELEN

Paris. Your son.

My husband.
                    (To PARIS, off)

You fool!
Can he hear?
                    (To PARIS)

Don't! Do not put
Down your sword! Nor bow!

What an idiot.
                    (To PARIS)

No! You need weapons! Not drink!

HECUBA

You married him.

HELEN

Aye.

I don't want him to
Die.

HECUBA

Perhaps fate does.

HELEN

What if?

HECUBA

What?

HELEN

What it he wins?

*They consider this for a
moment. They laugh.*

That doesn't sound right.

HECUBA

I've buried so many sons.
What's one more? Fate.

HELEN

Fate.

Perhaps I should—

HECUBA

Sh!
Relax. We should go inside.

HELEN

Perhaps we should go.

CHORUS OF TROJAN WOMEN

Are you watching this?
Hecuba doesn't waste time.
Wait! Something happens.

> *On the battlefield, PARIS*
> *hides and ACHILLES*
> *enters.*

ACHILLES
(Arguing with BRISEIS, off)

I'll be back when I'm
Done! I said, "I'll be back when
I'm done!" Be quiet!

You're distracting me.
That's why! Gods! A little faith!
That's all I'm asking!

I will come back there,
Briseis. I will come back
And will shut you up.

Go....Go....Go inside.
Inside. The tent. The tent. Tent.
You. Go inside. Tent.

Be...be...because I....
Because I said so! It is
My tent. Mine. Do not—

Do...Don't move...Don't move
Anything. No! I like it
The way it is! Gods!

My head aches. Woman!
Go inside. Because you're a
Slave. Yes. You're a slave.

No. You are not a
Princess. Not in my tent. I
Realize that you

Are not in my tent
Right now. But you are near it.
Near my tent, you're slave.

In Troy, you're princess.
In the Greek camp, you are slave.
I don't think you've quite

Got the concept! You
Are a slave girl. A prize. My
Prize! Slave! Obey me!

Go inside. Go! Go!
Inside and wait! All right. Stay
Outside, then. Just. Just.

Be quiet. I don't
Need…I don't need your advice.
Because I am the….

I am Achilles!
The age's greatest hero!
I don't need advice

On how to be the
Age's greatest hero! Gods!
I am! Really! They're

Already writing
Epics about me. I heard
On just yesterday!

While you were at the
Market! With Diomedes!
No. You can't ask him!

Look…Look…Stay…Stay there.
Quietly. I'm about to
Fight. Fight! With Paris!

Why do you think I'm
Out here? He's hiding! Behind
That rock.
                              (To PARIS)
          You can come

Out now. I see you.
                         (To BRISEIS)
I'll ask him!
                         (To PARIS)
          I'm Achilles.
You think you can hide

From me? Come on. Sit.
Sit! Is it a Trojan thing?
That you don't listen?

Sit.
                         (To BRISEIS)
          I will ask him!

                         (To PARIS)
So, how is Cassandra?

                         PARIS
          What?

                        ACHILLES
"What?" What "What"? You deaf?

How is Cassandra?

PARIS

How is Cassandra?

ACHILLES

Good boy.

PARIS

My sister, you mean?

ACHILLES

Is there another
Cassandra?

PARIS

I don't think so.

ACHILLES

Then that Cassandra.

How is she?

PARIS

She's fine?

ACHILLES

You don't know?

PARIS

I'm not sure how
To answer.

ACHILLES

Speak true.

PARIS

Truly. She is well.
She prays daily that the gods
Will take pity on

Their fair city and
Urge your hordes to return whence
You came. She mourns the

Loss of brothers and
Lovers and friends. She insists
That you Greeks will find

A clever ruse to
Cross our gates and slay our folk.
But that is absurd.

You've been here ten years.
She insists she won't live long
After the war ends.

But she is young. Yet
Fifteen. She'll be alive for
Years. So Cassandra

Sits inside, waits for
Peace and the chance to walk on
Pastures, smell the sea.

ACHILLES
(To BRISEIS)

She's fine!

(To PARIS)

    You didn't
Think I'd say all that, did you?
Now, where were we?

                              PARIS
Uhm.

                              ACHILLES
"Uhm"? You're about to
Die, and all you can think to
Say is, "Uhm"?

                              PARIS
          No. Uh....

                              ACHILLES
Again with the "uhm."

                              PARIS
More "uh," not "uhm."

                              ACHILLES
          You quibble?

                              PARIS
I do.

                              ACHILLES
          Very good.

Quibble away.

                              PARIS
          Thanks.

                              ACHILLES
          What?

                              PARIS
          What if...

                              ACHILLES
          Where?

PARIS

But....

ACHILLES

Who?

PARIS

Look....
I was wondering—

ACHILLES

Boo!

PARIS

Aah!

ACHILLES

Behind you!

PARIS

Where? What?

ACHILLES

It is the hydra!

PARIS

Help! Ho! The hydra!

Duck! That this fell beast
Should hunt me down and threaten
Me and my city!

What? Will you not hide?
Where is the hydra?

ACHILLES

It's dead.

PARIS

Did you kill it?

ACHILLES

No.

PARIS

Then who?

ACHILLES

Heracles.

PARIS

Who?

ACHILLES

Her-a-cles.

PARIS

What-e-ver.
Who the hell is he?

ACHILLES

Greece's greatest—well,
Second hero. Haven't you
Read our history.

PARIS

Why should I read of
Your pathetic culture? You
Can sack the cities

You will. Your culture
Will never amount to much.
Besides, until a

Few years ago, I
Was a shepherd, unlettered,
Simple. In a year,

I was prince and in
Sparta, with Menelaus'
Wife lying under

Me, begging for more.
I can still see her perfect
Breasts ripple as I

Thrust myself into
Her again and again, her
Legs wrapped around me,

Squeezing tighter, her
Cries echoing. To silence
Her, I had to clasp

My hands around that
Smooth throat so that no sound could
Escape to alert

Her loathsome husband.

                    ACHILLES
Are you quite finished?

                    PARIS
        That's what
She kept asking me?

                    ACHILLES
Paris. You. Me. Fields
Of Troy. You're about to die.
You wanted to speak.

                    PARIS
What if—

                    ACHILLES
        Duck!

                    PARIS
What? Where?

                    ACHILLES
I can do this all day.

        Will
You please just shut up!

                    ACHILLES
Brave words. Brave Paris.
Fine. Speak.

                    PARIS
        What if I should win?

                    ACHILLES
                    (Laughs)
I beg your pardon?

Wait! Wait! Deep breath. Calm.
All right. Again. Speak again.

                    PARIS
What if I should win?

                    ACHILLES
                    (Laughs again)
No. No. No. It's just
As funny the second time.
Where did you get...? What

Is that you're drinking?

                    PARIS
That's mine.

ACHILLES

Frisian courage
Good luck with that. Here,

Have more. Drink up. Look,
You seem nice enough, but I'm
Achilles. You die.

PARIS

That's it! Prepare to
Die!

*PARIS attacks
ACHILLES vigorously.*

Die you bastard! Die! Die!
Wait. Wait a moment!

Do you…think you could
Use your sword?

ACHILLES

No.

PARIS

Please.

He attacks again.

Come on!

He attacks again.

It's a rule. Come on!

ACHILLES

Why?

PARIS

Because it is
A duel. You have to use it.

He attacks again.

ACHILLES

Evidently not.

PARIS
(Out of breath)

Look. Take a breath. Calm
Down. Just. Moment. My wife and
Mother are watching.

ACHILLES

They on the wall?

PARIS

Yes.

ACHILLES

That's a nice piece. I'd like to
Stick her with my blade.

PARIS

That's my wife!

ACHILLES

No, no.
I meant your mother.

PARIS

That's wrong.

ACHILLES
(Waves toward the wall)

Hello!

PARIS

Leave her be!

He viciously attacks.

CHORUS OF TROJAN WOMEN

He waved at me. In
Your dreams. Woo hoo! Achilles!
Hush. He did not look

In your direction
At all. And he was looking
In yours? Yes. Why not?

If I'm going to
Get savaged, it should be by
A great hero. True.

P'rhaps he could savage
Us both. Together? He has
To savage someone.

HELEN

I shudder in fear!

HECUBA

Your skin is cold. Let's go in.
It will be warm there.

ACHILLES

What is it keeps her
With you? You're no warrior.
You'll never be king.

PARIS

What are you doing?
Stop that! Do…do not touch me.
Don't touch me! Help! Ho!

ACHILLES exposes
PARIS.

ALL
(Save PARIS, HELEN, ACHILLES, and AJAX)
Oh!

NESTOR
That explains a

Lot.

AJAX
What is it? I cannot

See.

ODYSSEUS
You don't want to.

HECUBA
Oh, you poor dear. Why
Don't we go inside? You can
Tell me your troubles.

HELEN
Explains why I stay.

HECUBA
No, no, dear. Beautiful child.
It is shame making.

CHORUS OF TROJAN WOMEN
The poets will have
Something to say 'bout Paris.
Gifted by the gods.

He stood before the
Might of the savage hordes and
Showed them Trojan strength.

The barbarians
Hang their heads in shame. Paris.
Our prince. Our hero.

ACHILLES

That is all right. I
Mean, nothing to be ashamed
Of.

PARIS

Ashamed? Of course

Not. Why should I be?

ACHILLES

Nothing wrong with it at all.
It is very…sweet.

PARIS

'Sweet'? Why say you 'sweet'?
I say it's magnificent!

ACHILLES

And you should. You should.

PARIS

Don't patronize me.

ACHILLES exposes himself.

Oh.

ODYSSEUS

Oh.

CHORUS OF TROJAN WOMEN

Oh.

CHORUS OF SOLDIERS

Oh.

HECUBA

Oh, dear.

BRISEIS

That's
Why I do not leave.

AJAX

That I can see.

HELEN   (Shrugs)

Eh.

CHORUS OF TROJAN WOMEN

Someone open the gates. They're
Already ope' wide.

HECUBA

Helen, dear. You should
Not have to watch this. Must be
Very distressing.

We should go inside.
The fire is warm. The wine spiced.
I can rub your feet.

CHORUS OF SOLDIERS

Poets will have more
To say of Achilles, who
Wields a mighty blade.

Beware, Trojans, his
Great spear. His thrust has conquered
Briseis and now

Must humble Paris.
It is great to be a Greek.
A Greek this fine day.

                    NESTOR

What are you talking

About?

                    CHORUS OF SOLDIERS
        Achilles' great sword,
His divine glory.

                    NESTOR

I don't see a sword,
Nor do I see glory.

                    CHORUS OF SOLDIERS
        How
Can you not see them?

                    NESTOR

How? Because his huge
Penis is in the way.

                    CHORUS OF SOLDIERS
        That's
What we were talking

About.

                    NESTOR

        If you mean
'Penis', say 'penis'. Do not
Talk around it. You

Will sound like one of
Those poets. Then you might as
Well put on a dress.

So, Achilles has
A large penis.

CHORUS OF SOLDIERS
Say not large.
Say magnificent.

NESTOR
That? Magnificent?
No. Now, Theseus had a
Magnificent cock.

Immensely proud of
It, he was. He would show it
To everyone.

PARIS and ACHILLES
fight.

ACHILLES
Would you like me to
Put away my shield? It might
Make the fight fairer.

He throws down his shield.
PARIS attacks.

BRISEIS
What is he doing?
Why does he toy with Paris?
Oh, he is cruel. Cruel!

ODYSSEUS
Even Achilles
Can stumble and fall. Ajax,
She may be yours yet.

AJAX

I cannot pray for
The fall of a comrade, e'en
If I benefit.

ODYSSEUS

Of course you can. Why
Not?

> *PARIS and ACHILLES*
> *fight.*

CHORUS OF GREEK SOLDIERS

It must be soon over.
The battle. The war.

> *PARIS and ACHILLES*
> *fight.*

> *ACHILLES stumbles and is*
> *slightly cut by PARIS.*

PARIS

Ah, ha! I mean.... Oh!
Sorry! I did not mean to hit....
Let me. I think the

Tunic can be cleaned.

> *ACHILLES punches*
> *PARIS.*

Ouch! What was that? Oh! My nose!
You broke my nose! Ass!

> *PARIS punches*
> *ACHILLES.*

It hurts, doesn't it?
So, now you know how it feels.

ACHILLES

Now, I'll use my sword.

PARIS

No! No! That's all right.
Why don't we call it even.
Just...you know.... Help! Ho!

Exit PARIS, pursued by
ACHILLES.

HELEN

His beautiful nose.

HECUBA

Why don't you take a hot bath?
I can scrub your back.

CHORUS OF TROJAN WOMEN

Paris sure can run
Fast. Where did he go? There! No.
There! He's so dreamy.

ACHILLES chases PARIS
across the battlefield as they
fight.

NESTOR

Now Jason's. That was
A magnificent cock. He
Could knock you off your

Horse just by turning
Around. You ever wonder
How Medea died.

Split in twain, she was.
Her father was quite put out.

(Muses)

Magnificent! Huge!

ACHILLES appears on the
battlefield.

ACHILLES

Paris! Paris! Where
Has that little toad hidden?
Listen, boy! I'll make

It fast. It will hurt,
But not too much! You have to
Stop running! I'm out

Of breath. That boy can
Run. This is no way to fight.
Not Greek, but Trojan

To fly instead of
Facing a foe. At the start
Of this war, Troy had

Men. They are all dead.
All the Trojan heroes dead.
Who's left to kill me?

No doubt, my death will
Be inglorious, will be
Unworthy. No point

In slaying insects.
No challenge. No joy. Perhaps
This will be my last.

There flies the noble
Paris, his fear leaving a
Stenched trail to follow.

He chases off.

BRISEIS

Ajax is a good
Man. Easy. Kind. Nor hero
Nor peasant. There is

Nor excitement nor
Fear with his kind. He is not
As clever as his

Friend, Odysseus,
Whose hard cold gaze frightens me.
Ajax might love me.

But he can never
Keep me. Live, Achilles! Live!
Come back to me, lord!

This time, there's something
In the air. That terrifies,
That terrifies me.

*ACHILLES chases PARIS
across the stage. ACHILLES
stops, sits, and waits as
PARIS runs off.*

NESTOR

Let me tell you of
Heracles. Minuscule. The
Smallest penis. You

Practically had
To have the damn thing in your
Face to see it. E'en

Then, you had to squint.
Boy, boy, was he proud of it.
He liked to go out

And about naked.
"I am Heracles!" he'd cry,
Waggling it about.

We all had to be
So impressed. Ridiculous.
Thought he was female

First time I saw him.
Went on a trip with him one
Time to Lerna. The

Finest bordello
Was there. Madam Hydra's! And
Heracles wanted

The nine best whores in
All the land. But they laughed at
Him. So, he cut off

Their heads and called for
More. Cut their heads off. In the
End, burned the place down.

After then, no sex
On campaign. What is the point
Of war without rape?

                                    *PARIS runs across the
                                    battlefield.*

ACHILLES

Stop!

PARIS does.

Stop! Catch your breath.
Better?

PARIS

Please! Please, don't kill me!
Look, you can have it.

Troy, I mean. Take the
Damn city. Stupid place. Take
It. Just let me live.

Do you want Helen?
Do you? I can arrange it.
I...I...I...I...don't

Want to die! Please don't
Kill me! What do you want? I'll
Do anything. E'en

That! Yes. Even that.
I learned some tricks from Helen.
If that's what you want.

Maybe a little
More wine first.

ACHILLES

Don't!

PARIS

I can!

ACHILLES

Don't
Touch me.

PARIS

I will!

ACHILLES

Don't!

HECUBA

How embarrassing,
To beg so for his life. Put
Your head there. That's nice.

PARIS

I am so depressed!
Imagine being married
To the loveliest

Woman in the world.
All she does is want. Want. Want!
And nothing I do

Is good enough. No.
We stand on the wall, and she
Points to this prince or

That hero always
To tell me how great they are.
How successful. How

Better than me. How
Not me they are. You don't know
What it's like to be

The ever failure.
Why even try? When I fail,
She gloats. If I should

Succeed, even some
Small vict'ry, it is never
Good enough for her.

And then there's mother.
What a bitch! She never lets
Go. She's the damn queen,

But am I allowed
Even to be a captain?
No! "Wouldn't be fair."

What's the point being
A prince? Just go ahead and
Kill me. Get it done.

                    ACHILLES

Gods! You're pathetic.
Let go. Let go of my leg.
I want to go. Home.

I'm going home. Home.
Away. Leaving these shores. You
Trojans can wallow

In your own filth, your
Own pointlessness, if you like.
Go burn in Hades.

                    PARIS

Take me with you.

                    ACHILLES

        Let
Go. I won't waste my steal on
The likes of you. Wretch.

                    ACHILLES leaves.

PARIS

I'm not even worth
Killing. Troy, not worth sacking.
What's become of us?

Are we fated to
Be forgotten, or worse, mocked?
I'll not stand for that.

Damn you, Achilles!
Damn you, Greeks! I am Paris.
I am prince of Troy!

I may not be wise
As Priam, brave as Hector.
I do have my pride.

Troy will rise, stand, fall.
But we will nor gather moss
Nor be forgotten.

No crumbling ruin.
Flame. Destruction. Victory.
Live or die Trojans.

PARIS picks up his bow and arrows.

Fools may condemn me.
I strike for my city, wife,

He shoots two arrows into the air.

And hope. Achilles!

ACHILLES turns.

ACHILLES

What is it now?

The first arrow strikes
ACHILLES.

Oh!
What foolishness is this?

The second arrow hits him.

Oh!
I'm struck and can't move.

This is no way for
Achilles to fall. Stand. Rise.
Strike back at this boy.

My arms will not move.
They will not lift the blade. Legs,
Carry me forward.

My body fails me.
Oh, infamy! Inglory!
Stand up! Strike! Fight on.

The air is chill. Comes
Paris now.

PARIS enters.

Coward!

PARIS

Could I
Have won sword to sword?

ACHILLES

Never.

PARIS

Then better
A live coward than dead fool.
Would you drink?

ACHILLES

Thank you.

> *PARIS gives ACHILLES a*
> *drink.*

My friends will come.

PARIS

I'll
Be gone ere then.

ACHILLES

Will you strip
My armor, my sword?

PARIS

I want naught of yours,
Greek. Naught save your departure
Or your death. You came

To sack my city.
Nor to claim it, nor usurp
Our trade, nor conquer

Our colonies. You
Saw our brilliance and you wished
To extinguish it.

> *PARIS shoots ACHILLES*
> *one more time.*

> *ACHILLES dies.*
>
> *PARIS hears the Greeks approaching and flees.*
>
> *ODYSSEUS, NESTOR, and CHORUS OF GREEK SOLDIERS enter.*

ODYSSEUS

Where is that bastard?

CHORUS OF SOLDIERS

On top of that hill. Get him!

> *A couple of arrows strike nearby.*

Duck! Duck!

ODYSSEUS

    Let him go.

NESTOR

Troy is ruined now.
We will have our vengeance.

ODYSSEUS

    Ere
This war is over,

Troy, her people, will
Cease to exist. Her language
Spoke only in hell.

What think you, Ajax?

CHORUS OF SOLDIERS
Where's Ajax? Where?

ODYSSEUS (Realizing)
Briseis!

Grab the kit but leave
The carcass. We go to the
Tent of Achilles.

They charge off.

CHORUS OF TROJAN WOMEN
Did not see that end
Coming. Paris will be back
Soon. Where to greet him?

Wait on the wall. First,
More wine. It's cool. Happy men
Will want to warm us.

They leave.

HECUBA
How could Paris win?

HELEN
I must inside. Paris comes.

HELEN exits.

HECUBA
What a disaster.

HECUBA leaves.

*BRISEIS in ACHILLES'
tent. AJAX enters.*

AJAX

We must go.

BRISEIS

   He's dead.

AJAX

Come to my tent. I can help
You there. Once you're there

You are mine.

BRISEIS

     You mean
Well, but you cannot keep me.

AJAX

E'en Odysseus

Will not break that law.

BRISEIS

Dear man. Dear Ajax.

AJAX

    I'll fight.
For you I will fight.

Know that.

BRISEIS

    I know, and
I love you for't. But you must
Know that you will lose.

That is my fate. Ne'er
To return to my home. Will
I e'en see sunrise?

Will the morning's warmth
Kiss my cheeks, the breeze comb my
Hair.

                         AJAX

    I will. I will.

                                        ODYSSEUS *is revealed*
                                        listening.

                         ODYSSEUS

How sweet.

                         AJAX

    Achilles
Gave her to me.

                         ODYSSEUS

    Did you not
Say that Achilles

Said that you could keep
Her only if I could not
Trick you? Outsmart you.

                         AJAX

He was joking.

                         ODYSSEUS

    Was
He? Nestor?

                         NESTOR

    Oedipus had
A normal penis.

In size at least. The
Things he could do with it. I
Always thought Jocast—

ODYSSEUS

We're not talking 'bout
Penises right now.

NESTOR

Why not?
What else is there to—

ODYSSEUS

Never you mind. What
Did you and I speak on?

NESTOR

Oh.
About Briseis.

ODYSSEUS

Yes, about her and....

NESTOR

Achilles' condition.

ODYSSEUS

Hear
That? His condition.

AJAX

Not condition.

ODYSSEUS

Yes.
Condition.

AJAX

No!

ODYSSEUS

Yes! Nestor?

NESTOR

Orpheus's bent,
Or twisted—

                              ODYSSEUS
        The matter at
Hand.

                              NESTOR
        Oh, yes. Of course.

I speak for the high
Kings. For Agamemnon. You
Obey, or see him.

                              ODYSSEUS
                            (To BRISEIS)
Ajax and I will
Roll for you.

                            (To AJAX)
        'Tis better this
Way.
                              AJAX
        How is it so?

                              ODYSSEUS
Were you to be sole
Possessor of such a rare
Treasure 't'would create

Discontent in the
Ranks. Can't be allowed. Shall we
Roll for our fair prize?

                              NESTOR
The high kings agree.

                    AJAX

He'll cheat.

                    ODYSSEUS
        You can choose the dice.
I'll put them down here.

                    AJAX

Briseis, you choose?

                    BRISEIS

What is going on? I was
Promised my freedom.

                    ODDYSEUS

You were promised to
Ajax. He was asked to free
You, but you are his.

Agamemnon, through
King Nestor, has allowed me
To challenge the gift.

I choose dice. Ajax,
Choose your dice.

                    AJAX

        I can't. You will
Cheat. Briseis, choose.

                    BRISEIS

Should I choose the dice
Placed before him?

AJAX

     Perhaps he
Anticipated

That. Our mistrust. P'rhaps
The weighted bones, are those he
Had given to me.

Put before me.

ODYSSEUS

     Choose.
Someone choose. I am a cheat.
I cannot but win.

AJAX

I pray to the shade
Of Achilles to help me.

BRISEIS

There are no more ghosts.

We must choose. You. I.
Those. I choose those.

ODYSSEUS

     Excellent!
Shall I roll, Ajax?

AJAX

Nay! Do not touch them!
He's too happy with your choice.

BRISEIS

I'll take the others.

ODYSSEUS

Most, most excellent.
Shall we roll?

                         BRISEIS
     Nay! See his eyes.
He is relieved.

                          AJAX
          He

Gave me the weighted
Bones knowing I'd not trust him.
Clever that. I'll take

The others.

                        ODYSSEUS
        Thank gods.

                         BRISEIS
Wait! What fiendishness is this?
What fresh evil now?

If I take those, I
Am damned. Odysseus and
The men will take me.

                          AJAX
If I choose those, I
Am doomed to lose you. He is
A monster!

                         BRISEIS
        Monster!

                        ODYSSEUS
They will not choose. Sad.

Nestor!

NESTOR

He used to strap it
To his ankle so

He could walk. The fool
Dislocated his hip when
First he laid eyes on

Thisbe. What a bitch.

ODYSSEUS

Old man! Ajax and the girl
Refuse to choose.

NESTOR

Then

They lose. Excellent.
Mind if I have a go?

ODYSSEUS

Be
My guest. Go first. I

Insist.

AJAX

But....

BRISEIS

But....

ODYSSEUS

But?
But. No buts. Take her away.

Exeunt, NESTOR and the
CHORUS OF SOLDIERS
leading BRISEIS.

You'll be better off.

AJAX

It is not fair. You
Cheated!

ODYSSEUS

    I cheat you? Ajax
You are my best friend.

All the dice were clean.

He produces a third set of dice.

These are the dice I cheat with.
Had you beaten me—

Odysseus the
Fox, the master cheat—the men
Would have known that the

Gods wished you to have
The lovely Briseis. Had
You lost and cried foul,

All would have believed
You. But you refused to play.
I had no choice, friend.

Here, drink Achilles'
Wine. Gods! Potent! Liquid fire!
Go by my tent. The

Black-haired bitch is there.
Her eyes look strange, but she is
Willing. Talented.

BRISEIS starts screaming
offstage.

Can you hear the men?
By the time they are done, you
Won't recognize her.

Or, just go back to
Your tent. Tend to your flock. I'll
See you tomorrow.

Here's Achilles' sword.
It must be worth something. And
In the morning, it

Will still be a sword.
I've no idea what she'll
Be.

*ODYSSEUS casually takes
the dice that had been placed
before him and rolls them, then
he leaves.*

*AJAX looks at the dice for a
moment. He takes his dice and
throws them.*

*He looks at the dice for a
moment, then hangs his head in
despair.*

                          AJAX
I would have won.

* * * * *

INTERMISSION

SCENE 5

THE WALLS OF TROY

*CHORUS OF TROJAN
WOMEN enter singing.*

CHORUS OF TROJAN WOMEN

"And Achilles falls!"
You're sharp. It is "Falls!" "Falls!" You
Are too high. Again.

"Falls!" "Falls!" Excellent.
"And Achilles falls!" I have
Got to sit down. My

Feet hurt. That's not all.
You're telling me! Those men are
Insatiable. Yes!

I am exhausted.
Maybe you should not sit, though.
Oh, you saucy bitch.

Glorious! To see
That man fall. To see the prince
Come into his own.

Did you see him? Near
Ares' temple about an
Hour past. A mad crush.

Even Priam was
Dancing in the streets. He grabbed
My ass! The old goat.

What do you think they
Are doing over there. They
Cringe and hide in fear.

We have Paris, you
Greek swine! Achilles' bane! Ha!
Send your best to die!

To die at the hands
Of our great hero. Greater
Even than Hector!

Yes. Kiss this, you scum!
That's nice. Yes. And they will not
Get their hands on mine.

                              Enter PARIS, drinking.

                    PARIS

Ladies! Ladies! Let
Us not disrespect the shade
Of great Achilles.

          CHORUS OF TROJAN WOMEN

Let us respect the
Person of noble Paris,
Who has lifted the

Veil of fear that has
Hung over our fair city
And clouded our hearts

For so many years.
You were magnificent. I
Saw you out there. Me,

Too! We were very
Impressed!

PARIS

Thank you, ladies. Whoa!
Look, but don't touch.

CHORUS OF TROJAN WOMEN

Not

Even a little?
A hero deserves some thanks.

PARIS

Maybe a little.

CHORUS OF TROJAN WOMEN

You were very brave.
You've made the Trojan people
Happy.

PARIS

They've been…kind.

CHORUS OF TROJAN WOMEN

We thought that you should
Be…rewarded by the right
Sort.

PARIS

That's…not…really…

Necessary.

CHORUS OF TROJAN WOMEN

It
Is. It is. It's our duty.
It is our pleasure.

PARIS

Well...I would not...Want
You...to be...deficient...in
Your...civic...duty.

CHORUS OF TROJAN WOMEN

Nor you in yours.

PARIS

No.
Wouldn't want...that.

CHORUS OF TROJAN WOMEN

You're a prince.

PARIS

So...noblesse...oblige.

CHORUS OF TROJAN WOMEN

How does it feel?

PARIS

Oh,
It feels...really...really...great.

CHORUS OF TROJAN WOMEN

Not that, you pig! Beast!

I really don't mind.
I meant to be a hero.
I didn't.

PARIS

Girls.... Girls!

Enter HECUBA.

HECUBA

Stop that this instant.

PARIS

I am handling it, mother.

HECUBA

No. They're handling it.

Go on, you garbage.
Get out of here.

CHORUS OF TROJAN WOMEN
    Caw! Caw! Caw!
Hail, Queen Hecuba!

HECUBA

Get out, or I'll give
You to the Ethiopes. Go!

*CHORUS OF TROJAN
WOMEN flees.*

Put that thing away.

PARIS

Mother!

HECUBA

    I am not
Impressed.

PARIS

    Mother!

HECUBA

    I've seen pricks
Before. Big pricks. Small.

Divine pricks. Mortal.
I'm nor impressed by the one
Between your legs, nor

By the one sitting
On this wall.

PARIS

Mother!

HECUBA

Oh, don't
"Mother" me, you puke.

Why could you not die?
Don't gawk at me you simp'ring
Moronic fool. Why

Could you not simply
Die? Achilles has spent the
Last decade mowing

His way through Trojans
And our allies. Troilus.
Penthesilia.

Hector. All killed by
This barbarian. Cities
Sacked. Whole armies slain.

But you, pathetic
And useless as you are, as
Villainous and as

Low as you are, you...
You somehow did not die. Why
Did my lovely son

Hector, child of hope—
Mine, his father's, his peoples'—
Have to die so young?

Why are you allowed
To wallow in decadent
Excess with your whore?

You have slipped and sleezed
Your way through life, into the
Heart of your father—

Feeble minded as
He is—and into the minds
Of the city's folk.

Somehow you've convinced
The ages' greatest tramp to
Run away with you.

Your life is lucky.
You have no skills. No talents.
Your blood, ill fated.

That you've lived so long
Is testimony to the
Fates' capricious whims.

This day, though, you were
Placed before the butcher, the
Perfect killer. How

Then, did you live? How
Is it that you slithered your
Slimy way from death?

That was the plan. That
Was the deal. One life. Just one
Putrid, useless life.

The Greeks have sat and
Lived and slept in their filth for
Ten years. All they want

Is an excuse to
Leave. I gave them one. No. Not
Helen, for what is

She. Oh, she's pretty.
But can Menelaus love
Again a woman

Who has cuckolded
Him so publicly? And so
Infamously? No!

He'll take her back to
Use, toss away like offal.
She can never be

Trusted. But he and
His brethren can ever hate
The man who stole her.

They will ever hate
The people who defend that
Man. You. They want you.

They want your carcass
Hanging like meat on their gates.
Then. Then, they will leave.

So, I promised them
You. Promised to deliver
You to Achilles.

Let their hero gut
You for their pleasure. Troy means
So much to me. It

Is the city of
Light, the home of my youth, my
Happiness as wife

And mother. As queen,
I've loved these people. I've loved
The very rocks and

Stones and bricks. I've loved
The cattle and the fields, the
Buildings and the roads.

What are you? Nothing.
Loathsome, contemptible, mean,
And petty. A boil.

A growth. A cancer.
Remove you, we could have healed.
We could have grown on.

Never trust a Greek.
I sent you out there, ready
For you to die. Die.

All you had to do
Was die. All Achilles had
To do was kill you.

The fool could not do
Even something that simple.
What have we done, I

Done to deserve one
Whom the deadliest killer
Fails to kill? What? What?

Pray, tell me. No. Do
Not open your foul mouth. Do
Not pollute my ears.

Your thoughts, your words, eat…
Gnaw at my soul. Be off with
You. Go back to your

Seed sodden sheets. To
Your willing whore. Do you think
That we do not know,

That we cannot hear
And see what depravities
You wallow in while

Troy crumbles, while our
People die, while my sons lie
Bleeding on the fields,

Sons, perfect, sublime?
So, you have slain Achilles.
Do you think that the

Greeks will forgive us?
Will they strike their tents and leave,
Depart defeated?

Will they absolve us
Of their humiliation?
Their shame? There can be

But one end now to
This war. Troy will burn. Fire. Death.
Men slain. Women raped.

Buildings toppled. Fields
Salted. Our stories e'en our
Civilization

Lost. Lost. Hecuba,
Forgotten. Hector, unsung.
Priam, rotting meat.

No one to bury
Us, to send our souls to their
Next lives. Our orphaned

Souls damned to weep on
These lifeless shores, by fallen
Homes. No gods will stand

For us. E'en Hades
Will bar his gates 'gainst us. All
Lost souls. Orphaned souls.

What did I do? How
Did I offend the fates, earn
Their contumely?

I know what. I bore
This abomination. I
Was warned. But mothers

Are fools. I should have
Aborted you. Not trusted
Some priest's potions, or

Wild animals. I
Should have taken the dagger
In mine own hands, placed

The bronze to my skin,
Sliced open mine own womb, pulled
Out the fetus and

Flung it against the
Rocks and ground it into the
Dust. I should have done.

Gods! Why have I not
The strength in these agéd hands
Yet to take his life?

Why've I not the will?
Harbinger of doom, why can't
You just die?

> *HECUBA leaves.*

> *PARIS sits for a long moment.*

                    PARIS
    Mother?

* * * * *

SCENE 6

THE GREEK CAMP

CHORUS OF SOLDIERS
enters.

CHORUS OF SOLDIERS

I am exhausted.
You? Four times. Four? Four. I could
But thrice. I think I

Tore a muscle. At
Least she stopped screaming. I think
Calchas shoved a cloth

In her mouth. I hope
He didn't kill her. Would not
Be as much fun, then.

She puts up a fight.
Maybe that's why Achilles
Liked her so much. P'rhaps.

He was a good man.
Achilles? Yes. One day, I
Was napping by that

Tree. Achilles had
Just killed some captain…someone.
So he walks back by

Me. He's covered in
Dust and blood and there was a
Piece of intestine

Hanging off his ear.
He comes up, Achilles does,
And kicks me in the

Ass. Kicks you in the
Ass? Yes. And he says to me,
"Get off your ass, you

Prick-eating bastard."
He called you a 'bastard'? A
'Prick-eating bastard'.

Wow! I know. I know!
And the kick in the ass! I
Knew I had to write

My wife about it.
What did she say? Nothing, I
Did not write to her.

Why not? Because, I
Do not know how to write. Oh,
That would explain it.

Why didn't you ask
Me? What? You could have asked me
To write her for you.

I did not know you
Could write. I can't, but it was
Rude of you not to

Ask. Really rude. I'm
Sorry. I didn't mean to
Hurt your feelings. It's

Mean. Presumptuous.
I'm sorry! I could ask…to
Make you feel better.

It's too late. Sorry.
That's all right. You didn't mean—
No, I didn't. Would

Not have made much of
A difference. No? No, I
Do not have a wife.

Ah. And if you did,
She probably would not be
Able to read. True.

I had a dog. Could
It read? I don't know. Never
Saw it read. Well, some

Dogs can be tricky.
I had to put it down when
I left home for here.

Sad, that. Yes. Though that
Makes the issue of whether
It could read, something

Of a moot point. Yes.
Could be useful, having a
Dog that could read. True.

Or a wife, for that
Matter. I fail to see an
Advantage to your

Wife knowing how to
Read. No, I meant just having
A wife. Expensive,

That's what wives are. Give
Me a captured slave girl. Don't
Have to feed them, for

One. Once you're done, let
Them go and starve in the cold.
And you can kill them.

If you want. Sometimes
That's for the best. Speaking of....
What's Agamemnon...?

No spears! No swords! You've
Already gone twice! She's ours!
We'd best get back there.

Should we tell Ajax?
He knows where she is. He can
Come if he wants to.

Enter NESTOR limping.

NESTOR

Gods! I've not ravished
Anyone like that in, what,
Thirty years or more.

We had gone to the
Frozen wastelands to the north.
Great hardy men there.

All heroes. All fell
To our strength and numbers. It
Was a good battle.

Like all great battles,
It was hard fought yet quickly
Won. No war should last

More than a few months.
Longer than that, the men are
Too tired and the slave

Girls begin to get
Scrawny. But those northern girls!
We spent months sailing

Along a river
Great and wide. A desolate
Place we found. Unloved

By Apollo's gaze,
Far from the path of his steeds'
Fiery journey.

So cold it became
That our morning's piss would freeze
Mid stream. Ha! We had

To snap it off like
A twiggy branch from a tree.
The men fought naked.

How they did that I
Do not even want to know.
Large, hairy men, all

Painted in bright hues.
They stood at the far edge of
The battlefield and

Howled and they raged, showed
Us their asses and waggled
Their cocks. Waggled them

At us. Scared the shit
Out of some of the men. Quite
Literally, in

Some cases. Butes,
His bowels opened up at
The sight. I did not

Know a man could hold
So much shit. Must have taken
Four or five minutes.

What a stench! Jason
Ordered the poor lad to bathe.
He never came back.

Anyway, had to
Admire the bald fools who stood
Naked in the snow.

Then, of course, had to
Kill them. A horde of naked
Men charging across

A field is a sight
Terrifying. Of course, then,
We realized that

They were naked. A
Terrible roaring's great, but
I'd prefer armor

Protected me and
You. Like slaught'ring helpless sheep,
It was. The wind was

Cold, but their blood warm.
Warmed you up, didn't it. Not
That you needed it.

Not once we reached their
Village. Oh! Oh, those women.
They were not naked.

At least at first. Ha,
Ha! We had the tall one with
The golden braids. Gods,

Did she enjoy a
Good fight. I broke two fingers
On my right hand. A

Couple of the men
Had to hold her down. Ha! Ha!
And she kept fighting!

Trying to bite me,
To gnaw off my face. So, I
Had to use the edge

Of my shield to shut
Her up. I did not mean to
Cut off her damned head.

But all that did not
Bother you, did it. You were
Magnificent. Yes.

You took her during
The afternoon, and in the
Night took her mother.

Then the next day, we
Found—you found—that little girl,
The one with the doll!

She was sweet. Kept her
Around for a few weeks. She
Kept crying, calling

For an 'äiti.'
"Äiti! Äiti!" What
A bother. Had to

Drown her. Only way
To shut her up. "Äiti!"
She was not so fun

After that. You were
A good friend. I thought I had
Lost you these last years.

Now I see you just
Had no reason to return.
Tonight, you came back,

Old friend. Thrice. And a
Good thrashing before the first.
Feisty girls. You like

Feisty girls. You were
Magnificent. Heroes here
Want poets to sing

Of their exploits. I
Would prefer they sing of yours.
Sing of Nestor's cock!

NESTOR'S SONG (Sings)

Pray to the gods and hide your daughters,
For Nestor's cock is here tonight,
Fa la la, fa la la. Derry derry derry doh.
For Nestor's cock is here.

Apollo, hang your head in shame-o,
While your Muses spread their legs-o,
Fa la la, fa la la. Derry derry derry doh.
For Nestor's cock is here.

Poor young Briseis screams and fights so,
My mighty thrust does shut her up,
Fa la la, fa la la. Derry derry derry doh.
For Nestor's cock is here.

Stand all you Greeks and cheer for Nestor,
Look on in envy at his might.
Fa la la, fa la la. Derry derry derry doh.
For Nestor's cock is here.

CHORUS OF SOLDIERS
and ODYSSEUS have been
watching.

ODYSSEUS, CHORUS OF GREEK
SOLDIERS, NESTOR (Sing)

Fa la la, fa la la. Derry derry derry doh.
For Nestor's cock is here.

Nestor's cock! Nestor's cock!
Mightiest cock in Greece—
Trojans fear, women groan—
Conqueror of the weak.

ODYSSEUS (Sings)

Nestor was such an ancient hero,
No one thought the thing would work-o,
Fa la la, fa la la. Derry derry derry doh.
For Nestor's cock is here.

He rose tonight to the occasion,
He took Briseis—first in line,
Fa la la, fa la la. Derry derry derry doh.
For Nestor's cock is here.

Screams we have heard and so have wondered
What has this ancient Nestor done?
Fa la la, fa la la. Derry derry derry doh.
For Nestor's cock is here.

Bruised and battered is fair Briseis,
Testimony to Nestor's might,
Fa la la, fa la la. Derry derry derry doh.
For Nestor's cock is here.

ODYSSEUS, CHORUS OF GREEK
SOLDIERS, NESTOR (Sing)

Fa la la, fa la la. Derry derry derry doh.
For Nestor's cock is here.

Nestor's cock! Nestor's cock!
Mightiest cock in Greece—
Trojans fear, women groan—
Conqueror of the weak.

CHORUS OF SOLDIERS (Sing)

Nestor's a king we want to follow.
He'll give us lots of lusty whores.
Fa la la, fa la la. Derry derry derry doh.
For Nestor's cock is here.

He breaks his fingers as he beats them,
Making it easier for us.
Fa la la, fa la la. Derry derry derry doh.
For Nestor's cock is here.

Though Nestor must be over eighty,
He rapes like a lad of twenty.
Fa la la, fa la la. Derry derry derry doh.
For Nestor's cock is here.

When I am old I want to be like
The Nestor we have seen tonight.
Fa la la, fa la la. Derry derry derry doh.
For Nestor's cock is here.

ODYSSEUS and CHORUS OF GREEK SOLDIERS (Sing)

Fa la la, fa la la. Derry derry derry doh.
For Nestor's cock is here.

Nestor's cock! Nestor's cock!
Mightiest cock in Greece—
Trojans fear, women groan—
Conqueror of the weak.

Fa la la, fa la la. Derry derry derry doh.
For Nestor's cock is here.

ODYSSEUS (Sings)

Nestor's cock!

CHORUS OF SOLDIERS (Sings)

Nestor's cock!

ODYSSEUS and CHORUS OF SOLDIERS (Sing)

Mightiest cock in Greece.

ODYSSEUS (Sings)

Nestor's cock!

CHORUS OF SOLDIERS (Sings)

Nestor's cock!

ODYSSEUS and CHORUS OF SOLDIERS (Sings)

Mightiest cock in Greece!

NESTOR (Sings)

My Cock!

ODYSSEUS, CHORUS OF GREEK
SOLDIERS, NESTOR(Sings)

Nestor's cock!

ODYSSEUS

Well sung, ancient king.
Take him, men, for his job is
Not yet finished. Lift

Him on your shoulders.
Take him. He goes where many
Have already gone.

They leave.

* * * * *

SCENE 7

AJAX'S TENT

*AJAX is alone, feeding his
sheep and drinking —
continuously*

AJAX

Here you go, small one.
Briseis wanted to meet
You. To play with you.

Leave him alone. Let
Him eat. Here is food for you
Here. Here you go. Do

You want more? Then take
It, damn it! Damn you all! No.
No! Do not be scared.

I…I'm…just upset.
That's all. What is wrong with me?
I could have stood up

To Odysseus.
Why not? I'm as good as he.
I am stronger. So

Many men, Greek and
Trojan, have marveled at my
Strength, feared my power.

Yet I could not stand
Up to Odysseus. I'm
Not as smart as he.

I could have said, "No!
No, Odysseus! The girl's
Mine. By gift! By right!

There are other slaves
For you. Younger. P'rhaps fairer.
Go your way and leave

Briseis to me.
As friend to Achilles—yes,
I was his friend if

He'd any—I claim
Her. As Achilles gifted
Me her, I claim her.

As king, I claim her.
As a warrior who has
Time and again stemmed

The Trojan tide and
Saved these ships, I claim her. As
I am alone, my

Family, people,
Friends are dead or far away,
I claim Briseis.

As I love her, I
Claim her, and with my heart so
Promise to keep her.

As you are my friend,
As you love me, I claim her!"
But you can't let me.

A decade o'ercast
And gray brings me one ray of
Sunlight, and you must

Take it. From me. Friend!
Great Ajax. Ajax the fool.
As fool, I lose her.

I cannot say it.
My tongue stumbles and you take
My most precious prize.

I've abandoned my
Kingdom for this pointless war.
My people, who loved

Me, perhaps obeyed
Me, at least they feared me. Who
Do they fear, obey,

Love now? Has some fool
Seduced my nagging horrid
Wife and usurped both

My bed and my throne,
All for this pointless war. The
Young of my lands fed

To the ravenous
Gods of slaughter, for who else
Had benefited

From this pointless war?
Friends butchered, youth spent, money
Gone, fields fallow, my

Cities crumbling in
Neglect. All for a pointless
War o'er Spartan whore.

One chance for hope, for
Happiness. Fair Briseis.
She could have loved me,

Could have been one thing
Good to come from this pointless
War. Now. Now. Nothing.

No one to return
To. No one to take back. No
One to fight for. A

Dead man's sword. Blood soaked,
Drenched in lives and tempered in
Death. 'Tis valuable.

Too valuable to
Sell. Haunted by the pain of
Innumerable

Victims. Hated by
The gods, save Hades, who feasts
On the meat butchered

By its sharp edges.
Do the gods loathe me as well?
Do they look down from

High Olympus and
Despise me for my weakness?
For my cowardice?

Does Achilles' shade
Condemn me? Who is he to
Condemn me? He who

Lost to frail Paris.
What fool was he to give her
To one who'd lose her.

How dare you? How could
You leave lovely Briseis
To Odysseus

And his band of thieves
And cutthroats? You knew. You had
To know they'd take her.

How they've taken her.
The screams so stabbed at me I
Could barely stand it.

I wanted to tear
My ears from mine own head to
Stop the screams, the noise.

So I sat here. Sat
And heard the beasts at their sport.
Watched them laugh and play

As they waited their
Turns. Watched them boast their conquests,
Knowing that had I

The courage, will, I
Could have taken her. I still
Could. Couldn't I? Could

I? My strength is no
Match for Odysseus' wit
Or ancient ally

Nestor. Nestor! You
Too have harmed my lovely girl.
Do you laugh at me?

Do you mock me, sir?
I am Ajax! I am king
As well as you! Who

Are you to scoff at
Me? You old crow. You withered
Cock! You feebled reed!

Waves of Trojans have
Broken on the rock that is
Ajax. I have faced

The fury of foes
From an hundred diff'rent lands,
While you have dried up

And shriveled in your
Sumptuous ease. I merit!
I have earned the right

To my prize! My prize
That you have glibly stolen
From me! You're a thief!

Do not look at me!
Do not laugh! Stop laughing! Stop!
Away with your pruned

Smirk, your wrinkled smile!
Leave off your cackling. I swear
By Achilles' blade—

My consolation—
I will have my vengeance, my
Satisfaction. Mine.

Be gone Nestor or
Die! I'm warning you! I am
Ajax and do not

Jest where death's concerned.
Leave off, or I'll cut you! Go
Away! Have at you.

AJAX slashes out with
ACHILLES' sword. There is
an ovine shriek.

There's Nestor, drowning
In his own blood and filth. Who
Else? Who else would die?

You, Menelaus.
You started this slaughter in
Anger at your wife's

Adultery, yet
You would so abuse my prize,
My flower, my love.

You have impaled her,
So I impale you with steel.

He strikes out again to further
ovine screams.

Thus, Menelaus!

Diomedes. Friend
To Achilles. You would so
Abuse his will? Nay!

He strikes again. More
screams.

I say nay! And you,
Agamemnon. The last sound
You hear will be my

Roar, The last sight my
Smirk!

AJAX is now swinging wildly.
Each attack is accompanied by
a cry.

      I do not care whom you
Serve. Which king. Which god.

I will strike you down.
You shall not withstand my rage.
Save Odysseus.

I will not stain my
Blade with your blood. Runt that you
Are, I shall tear you,

Rend you limb from limb
With my bare hands. Die you foul
Ithacan. Die! Die!

He tears apart a screaming
lamb.

So lies the Greek host.
Victim to Ajax's wrath!
I spit on you. I

Drink your very blood.
I piss on your carcasses.
Poets, sing on that!

No more Greek host. No
More humiliation. No!
Tired Ajax is spent.

AJAX embraces
ACHILLES' sword. He is
drained, drunk, and falling
asleep.

Oh, Briseis. How
Cold you are. Let me warm you.
Come and lie with me.

Come lie with me. You
Are my love, my wife. I will
Ever hold you dear.

Let the sun rise to
See the remains of Greece's
Might. Let it witness

What Ajax will do
For love. Dear Briseis, lie
With me. Embrace me.

Let our lips taste each
Other, our hands entwine and
Our hearts beat as one.

Tomorrow will we
Face tomorrow. Tonight, we
Will sleep, sleep in peace.

* * * * *

SCENE 8

THE TROJAN WALLS

PARIS enters. He has been drinking heavily.

PARIS

Why can't I just die?
Why would anyone want that?
I am not so bad.

Had I not taken
Helen, someone else would have.
It just happened to

Be me. I did not
Do it on purpose. Why does
Ev'ryone blame me?

The Greeks are like a
Cancer. Growing, destroying
All in their paths. They

Would have turned their pale
Eyes towards our golden city
Sooner or later.

How many peoples
Have they ridden down? Towns razed?
The roads have been clogged

For decades by the
Refugees. Like a cancer,
Greeks destroy us, yet

Leave naught in our place.
Someday. Someday, the Greeks will
Find no more lands to

Conquer, and perhaps
Then, their fury, their armies,
Will wither on the

Vine and die. Perhaps.
Perhaps culture will again
Thrive and another

Troy will rise. P'rhaps. Will
We be forgot? Will Hector's
Tale be sung or not?

Will Helen's beauty
Inspire poets, or will it
Attract ridicule?

And what will be my
Repute? What will be Paris'
Reputation? How

Will they judge me? Who
Will the judges be to bend
Their thoughts, their scorn, t'wards

This ill-fated place?
Maybe another city
Will rise, founded by

Whatever fools, or
Wise men, escape Greek-lit flames.
That city will rise,

And, like Troy, be a
Light, be a beacon, for the
Ages. Like Troy be

A great culture, be
The envy of the world, a
Home to invention,

Art, poetry, a
Home for beauty and wisdom.
Great kings will lead her.

Great minds will foster
Greater thought. What will they say
Of me? Will they mock

Me as well? Will they
Also be overrun by
Barbarian hordes?

Will their culture, too,
Be dismantled, razed? Or, will
It live on through time?

What of Paris then?
Is there nor time nor people
Who will not loathe me?

I've slain the greatest
Of heroes. Will I remain
The ever fool? I?

I should be recalled
As the lover. Must I be
The cretin always?

P'rhaps I should have died.
One moment of blinding pain,
Then all'd be over.

Now I live in fear.
What do the Fates have in store
For me? What future?

Shall I watch my love
Taken, handed to the troops,
Used like a slave whore?

Or are the Fates more
Cruel? Helen. Raised up. Lauded.
Made queen once again.

Her beautiful face
Looking down on my corpse, my
Humiliation.

Smirking. Thriving. Does
She, will she, laugh at the doom
Of so many who

Have suffered for her?
Will she mock Paris as well?
Vile bitch to mock me!

What life is there, what
Hope or joy without Helen?
How cruel the Fates would

Be to part our souls
Even in death. Trojans, you
May condemn me! Greeks,

You may slay me. But
Helen, my destruction lies
In you! Without you,

What can Paris be?
I'm nothing. A hopeless fool.

(Yawns)

Sleep, drink, take me now.

Take me someplace where
There is hope, where there is peace,
Where there is Helen.

PARIS *sleeps.*

Enter *HELEN.*

HELEN

So, Paris slumbers,
This tragedy's author lies
Asleep in own filth.

For you, I have lost
All. I have lost, abandoned,
My family, my

Husband, my homeland.
Because of you, thousands of
My people lie dead.

I can see, smell, their
Bodies rotting on the fields,
Fields that will never

Again know life, know
Beauty. I've watched from these walls
And seen my cousins,

Childhood friends, be cut
Down, hacked to pieces. I've stood
And listened to them

Cry out in pain, beg
For mercy where there is none.
I have seen my new

Family die, be
Wiped out, hunted down, destroyed.
All because of you.

My new city is
A ruin, is a ghost town.
The men, gone. Women,

Wasted. death hangs o'er
Ev'ry home. I taste it e'en
In food and water.

All because of you.
So much death and destruction.
Because of Paris.

What sorcerer's spell
Have you cast on me? What have
You promised the gods?

You are no great king.
You are no great warrior.
You are no poet

Or philosopher.
You are one princeling among
So many others.

You are crass, vulgar.
You are a mean and petty
Bully. You hide 'hind

These walls while others—
Braver, stronger—defend your
Marital priv'lege.

You wallow in your
Filthy luxury while your
People dig through filth

In hope of a scrap
Of food. They freeze, while you, we,
Soak in steaming wine.

You are faithless and
Lazy, dull and stupid. You
Are nothing. A null.

I despise you with
All of my soul. The mere thought
Of you makes me sick.

Why is it, then, that
I love you with all of my
Heart? When you're away,

I can hate you. In
My mind, I tell you how I
Feel. In my mind, I

Can free myself from
You and fly from this city
Of misery. In

My mind, I have my
Honor, my reputation.
But then I see you.

How can I love you
So much? Why do I long for
You, your kiss, your…touch…?

The touch of…your hands…
Of your…fingers…excites…me….
When you…caress…me…

The skin…my face…mouth…
My throat…my breasts…my thighs…my….
I can…feel…your…strength….

Can feel your...power....
What...spell have you...? What...magic...?
That you can.... Hold...me...!

That you can...give me
Such...pleasure....? Can't...can't...resist....
Cannot...not...deny...!

I need more...always
More...more...Again and...again.
Hold me! Paris! Take...

Me! Master me...! Make
Me beg...Make me...cry out! Oh!
Then leave me sated.

Sated but never
Satisfied. Not completely.
Oh, my love! How can

I want your death? How
Can I abide that you live?
Can't live without you.

Each second, ev'ry
Moment with you is both joy
And horror. Love, hate.

Laughter, tears. Life. Death.
Why do the Fates so hate me?
Why do they curse me

With you, you lovely
Man? My man. My damnation.
My terror. My heart.

Hecuba's plan made
Sense in comfort of her couch.
One quick death. I'm free.

Troy is free. You're dead,
Of course. But there is a price
To be paid for peace.

It seemed so easy.
So many times I almost
Told you of the plan,

Warned you. When we lay
Together. When you let me
Touch you, pleasure you.

I wanted to cry
Out, "Don't go beyond the gates!
Stay...with...me! In...me!

Take me...husband! Take
Me...! Lover! Pinch my cheeks! Tear...
My flesh...Into the

Dirt! Pound me into
The dust...Hurt me...me...like the
Whore...that...I...am! Oh!

Gods, why do you loathe
Me? What have I done to earn
Such ignominy?

Whom have I sinned 'gainst?
Or is't my father? Mother?
What are the sins that

You punish? Gods! Fates!
Take me ere Paris takes me
Again! If not his,

Then let my life be
Forfeit! Let me die! Kill me!
Let history, let

The poets piss on
Me! Stop this holocaust! Stop
This pain! Their pain. Mine.

But, no. There is no
Easy exit for Helen.
Beauty is my gift.

Beauty is my curse.
My lover will die. My friends.
My city. My hope.

So, Helen will age.
Time will have her jest. Helen
Will wither and fade.

They'll remember the
Face. Remember the beauty.
Forget all the rest.

PARIS stirs.

PARIS

Helen.

HELEN

   Love.

PARIS

   Sweetheart.
Kiss me. No, no! Not there. Kiss
Me. Yes. There. Yes! Oh!

* * * * *

SCENE 9

AJAX'S TENT

AJAX still sleeps. By and by, he awakens. It is dark in the tent.

AJAX

Briseis! Brise…!
Is't not my lady? 'Tis not.
'Tis Achilles' blade.

My blade, now. My sole
Inheritance from the dead
Hero. It was his

Gift that in the night
Cut me. And is Achilles'
Wine that now cuts me,

Slices into my
Very thoughts. Yet combined, they
Do not dull the pain

Of having lost my
Briseis. Gods, though, how they
Try. Oh, how they try.

What is the time? Should
I ope' the curtains and brave
The sun's stabbing rays?

Should I remain in
Dark's embrace and hang onto
Last night's dreams, in them

Did I embrace my
Briseis, and did she hold
Me in her soft arms.

She was not target
To the lustful attentions
Of the others but

Was the object of
My undying love—not their
Rough caresses but

My gentlest touches.
What beauty is there sometimes
In dreams. And terrors.

In slumber's journey
I fought a great host. Dozens
Of mine own allies

I met and battled.
E'en sneaky Odysseus
Could not avoid my

Fell blade. I emptied
These filthy beaches of this
Putrid host, cov'ring,

Drenching them with blood.
All to save Briseis. All
To save her. So should

I remain in the
Dark. Close my eyes to dull the
Thunderous throbbing

That chases me from
My sleep. Close my eyes and once
Again journey to

A land, a wondrous
Place where Briseis reigns and
Our enemies die.

What a glorious—
What's this? It smells, tastes of blood.
Has someone…? Is that

Hirsute Antiphus?
What do you here? There are more!
By the size of your

Arms: Leonteus.
Meges. That must be you, and
You, Agamemnon.

What great battle was
There? If only I could see
The field of conflict.

Ah! This runt must be
Odysseus. Ersatz friend!
Who's had the last laugh?

So, dead Greeks, where is
My Briseis? Does she wait
For me? Briseis!

Lady! Have all the
Deaths scared you? Are there other
Greeks who violate

You? I will kill them
As well. I will face what kings
Remain. I will face

The judgment even
Of the gods with clear conscience
If I can save you.

Apollo, cast your
Eyes upon Ajax' fury
And its consequence!

*AJAX opens the tent flaps letting in the
morning sun.*

What's this? Psipsino!
Who has done this to you? Who?
Mwaki-mu, where are….?

There. So brutally
Cut down with the others. What
Horror! What horror!

Where is…? Where is…? There.
Little lamb! Such a small thing.
Golden and perfect.

Who did this? I did.
I did it. I remember,
Though my memory

Is cloudy, I can
See the slaughter through the haze.
I did it. Blinded

By liquor most foul!
Because of my misguided
Love, I have slain the

Only creatures who
Ever loved me. Innocent,
Pure as they were, now

They are dead. What fear
They must have known, in the night,
To have seen my rage,

For my wrath to have

Been their last sight. Oh, Ajax,
What a fool you are.

Little lamb, I am
So sorry. Just yesterday
You gamboled about

This place, desperate
To escape, explore the world,
And now you are most

Cruelly killed by my
Hands. Why have the Fates done this?
Done this to Ajax?

While you were alive,
I e'er had companionship.
Now, I'm all alone.

Now, I'm all alone.
Little lamb, forgive me. So
I can forgive me.

Can I forgive me?
Does Ajax merit solace?
Deserve forgiveness?

Or is punishment
Living on alone? Without
You. Worse—without her.

BRISEIS has been watching
for some moments. She is
shrouded and can barely move.

BRISEIS

They were lovely.

AJAX

    Yes.
Lady, they certainly were.

BRISEIS

I wish I'd known them.

AJAX

They knew you, lady.
I spoke of you to them. I
Told them how gentle

And lovely you are.
I brushed them with what I thought
Would be your gentle

Touch. But these are not
The hands of a princess but
Of a monst'rous beast.

BRISEIS

Say not so!

AJAX

    I do!
Look what I have done to them,
Whom I loved but a

Fraction as much as
I loved—love—you.

BRISEIS

    You loved me?

AJAX

Can you e'en doubt it?

I have loved you, with
All of my heart, with all of
Mine own honor. To

Your dishonor, to
My shame. For your pain, your fate
Were as much my fault,

My doing, mine, as
Those foul men's.

BRISEIS

Nay. Say not so.
You could not stop them.

AJAX

I could have tried. I
Should have tried.

BRISEIS

You'd have been slain
For trying. They were

Madmen. You could not
Have stopped them.

AJAX

Achilles would
Have

BRISEIS

Achilles lies

Rotting on a dead
Field. Achilles ruled through fear.
He lost to a fool

Too drunk, too stupid
To know fear. Perhaps even
Achilles would not

Have stood up to the
Lust-blinded host of Greece that
Took me. You were wise.

                              AJAX

I was afraid.

                            BRISEIS

          P'rhaps
There's wisdom in fear.

                              AJAX

          There is
Cowardice as well.

                            BRISEIS

Then be the coward.
Be the coward, be alive.
What good t'me's your death?

                                                        Pause.

                              AJAX

I do love you still.

                            BRISEIS

No!

                              AJAX

          Yes!

                            BRISEIS

          I say, no.

AJAX

I say
Yes. I love you. I.

I love you and if
You will, I will keep you. It
Is my right. It is

My pleasure. Lustful
Soldiers cannot take love from
Me. I can take you

From here. Some place. There
Must be some island where we
Can be. We can lie

On the beach and laugh
And pretend there never was
Neither Greece nor Troy

Nor Achilles nor
War. There is only you, me.
My people are naught.

My wife, forgotten.
My throne can sit empty, for
All I care. I will

Face the scorn of the
Greeks, the enmity of great
Kings. I care not. For

You, I care and will
Do all, sacrifice all. Lose
All. For I love you.

Lady Briseis,
Let me be your lord. Let me
Spend eternity

Making up for your
Pain. Let us fly this evil
Place. Let us enjoy

Our youth and revel
In your beauty and my strength.
Let's age together.

Lov'ly Briseis,
Fear not my wrath, my sword, my
Soldiers, even my

Reputation. I
Will put aside my martial
Inclinations. My

Sword, my arm, my wealth,
My brawn serve only you. I
Know no general

Save you. You are the
Mistress of my hopes, dreams, e'en
Fears, for I love you.

BRISEIS

Stay!

AJAX

     Do not ask that
I stay my heart.

BRISEIS

     I ask that
You do stay your tongue.

I have no doubt that
Your oaths and promises are
Sincerely proffered.

AJAX

I swear on what I
Have left of honor that I
Will spend the rest of

My days with you if
Only each day begins and
Ends with lover's kiss.

BRISEIS

I cannot accept
Such a debt from one who is
So dear to my heart.

AJAX

My soul thrills to hear
You speak thus, and so again
I plight you my troth.

BRISEIS

I beg you listen.
I have faith in your sweet words.
But your comrades, they

Were not so gentle
In last night's ministrations.
Rough touch begets rough

Touch. Struggling was
Met with discipline. Quiet
Acquiescence sparked

Anger. They did not
So much take Briseis as
Stormed Troy. They sacked Troy

With a fury, with
Abandon, ten years of pent
Up rage spent in one

Night. You must look, dear
Ajax, and see what they've left.

AJAX

I know that I will

Still love you. No man
Can mar your beauty so. I
Am a warrior.

I've seen scars and cuts,
Amputations. I have seen
Mutilations. I

Know what man can do.
I have done it myself. There
Are many Trojans

And other foes who,
Living or dead, wear my brand.
I've offered you my

Heart, dear Briseis.
To the sweet girl I knew in
Hero's tent, and the

Wonderful woman
Who has been so abused, to
My everlasting

Shame. I owe you, my
Love. My heart. Mine honor. My
Word. What is your will?

BRISEIS

I will hold you to
Your word.

AJAX

I pray that you will.

BRISEIS

But first, you must look.

Turn, dear Ajax. Face
Sun's rays. Face heart's hope, and with
Apollo, see what

I have become. Then
Will I hold you to your word. See
What has been done.

*She removes her shroud. She
has been brutally, cruelly, and
indescribably ruined.*

AJAX

Gods!

BRISEIS

Gods! Gods! You said "Gods!"
What mortal man could do this?
What man would do this?

None! None. Only the
Gods have such hatred for their
Creations. What sins

Am I to blame for,
Mine or my ancestors, I
Do not know, nor do

I want to learn. I
Shudder at the very thought.
To punish me so

Would require the gods
To look on me, and even
Hades would balk at

Having me in Hell.
Is there even enough gold
To bribe dark Charon

To let me on his
Ferry? Even Cerberus
Would bolt, his demon

Tail tucked twixt his legs.
Achilles' shade would quail and
Lesser ghosts would flee.

Last night, terrorful
As it was, was naught to what
My future must be.

E'en death will bring no
Solace, save…save…the gift I
Can give you, dear one.

I have no fear that
You would break your promise to
Me. Indeed, my fear,

My terror, is that
You would stand by me, love me.
Yet ev'ry morning

You would see what I
Have become. Do not speak. You
Recoil to see me.

In every look,
In every embrace, with
Ev'ry glance, there will

Be revulsion. Dear,
How can I demand your love?
I who make you retch!

In my heart, I know
The tenderness, peace, and joy
I'd have given you.

Yet I know that is
No longer possible. No.
Our days, and our nights

Will be overwhelmed
By my hideousness. I
Cannot ask that of

You, my dear Ajax.
For your love would soon become
Hatred, resentment.

I beg and pray that
I might be able to close
My eyes, and in my

Mind see your goofy
Loving gaze smiling at me,
Not the shock and fear

I see before me
Now. I want you to see my
Beauty in your dreams.

I want you to want
Me, to long for, yearn for me,
My youth, my body.

Close your eyes. Can you
See my smooth skin, see my bright
Smile, welcoming breasts?

See them. Remember.
You have oathed your obeisance.
I demand two things.

I make two wishes.
One that you let me remain
Young and beautiful

In your eyes and your
Memories. The other that
You let me do so

In mine. Dear Ajax,
I beg, I demand, that you
Let me help me die.

AJAX

Dearest Briseis!
I cannot—

BRISEIS

  You must. I pray!
What future is there

For me? What peace left?

*BRISEIS takes
ACHILLES' sword and
places it in AJAX's hands.*

Take Achilles' sword, your sword.
Hold it. Embrace me,

And in that embrace,
Let your sword consummate our
Love.

AJAX

Let me take you—

BRISEIS

Had we but met in
Another time, dear Ajax,
In another place.

P'rhaps we'd be happy.
Perhaps we'd be together
'Til the end of days.

But we met now, and
Here your great love found love in
Curséd Briseis.

Embrace me, Ajax.
With your fell sword deflower
My mortality.

AJAX

Dear lady! I can—

BRISEIS

No words. Hold me quick. Take me!
I can feel no pain!

She throws herself on the blade.

One kiss, my darling.
A first kiss for our love. A
Last kiss for farewell.

They kiss.

Had we but met in
Another time, my dear friend,
In another place.

BRISEIS collapses and is still.
AJAX lowers her to the floor.

AJAX

Had we but met in
Another time, sweetest love,
In another place.

Let me cover you,
For the air is cool. Is it
Morning or death's chill

I feel? I shall warm
You. Sleep, dear one. Sleep with friends
Who love you. Sleep well.

Sleep softly, for you
Shall not be alone for long.
Be warm. Lie quiet.

Had we but met in
Another time, dearest love,
In another place,

There would be no great
Princes to keep us apart,
No kings to mock me.

There would be no war
To spoil the freshness of morn's
Gentle kiss on your

Brow. Nor Trojan tricks
Nor Greek stratagems to keep
Evening's breeze from

Brushing your hair. My
Lady would know no tears, would
Know nor death nor pain

Nor hunger nor fear.
There would be no more hurt. There
Would be no more death.

Had we but met in
Another time, Briseis,
In another place,

Our obligations
Could not, dare not, hinder our
Love, would not rear their

Heads and cry out, "Hold,
Lovers! For we have need of
You, your happiness.

It belongs to us!
We shall not give it back for
Your life, your joy, your

Salvation!" No, no,
Dear lady. All debts would be
Paid. We would be free!

Had we but met in
Another time, dear lady,
In another place,

I would take you in
My arms, carry you to the
Highest mountain tops,

And tell the world how
Much I love, I need, I yearn,
For you, dearest one.

I could hold you in
My arms, and when you slept, I
Would watch over you.

I'd happily spend
My days and nights on my knees
Worshipping you, for

You are my goddess!
I spit on Aphrodite,
Hera, Athena.

Their pale charms bring naught
But pain, misery to so
Many. But you. One

Smile could light the hearts
Of an empire. Your laughter,
Leaping from your heart,

Spreads throughout the skies
Causing the constellations
And the distant stars

Far out there, beyond
The grasp of Zeus himself, the
Sound brings lost souls warmth.

Your softest touch, your
Gentlest caress could fill me
With such joy that I

Would leap and gambol
By the dancing sea and sing!
Tra la la! Tra la!

Tra la la. Tra la.
Those words you will never hear.
Tra la la. Tra la.

Had we but met in
Another time, my heart's love,
In another place.

Had we but met in
Another time, sweet lady,
In another place.

Yet, we did not. We
Met now, here. Here and now, we
Stand on opposite

Sides of a great gulf
Of enmity. We met here,
Surrounded by war,

Disease, death, despair.
We met here, where the roar of
Hatred drowns the sweet

Sounds of love. We met
Here, where blood drowns all beauty.
We met here. And now.

When hearts are ruled by
Greed and envy and spite and
No one cares for love!

To my shame, I was
Once a man with such a heart.
If I could tear it

From my breast and give
You peace and beauty with it,
I'd gladly do so.

I must cast off this
Warlike countenance, reject
The monster I have

Become. I do this
For you. I know not what paths
You follow now, where

Your journey takes you,
What shades or demons guide you.
But I will find you.

I will keep you, and
Together we will face what
Evils Hades has

In store for us. Ere
I take your hand, I must 'gain
Achilles' blade take

Up.

*AJAX holds the point of the
blade against his chest. There is
a long hesitation.*

      I have not your
Courage, my love. Ajax knows
Fear. I sacrifice

All for you. Will you
Be there so we together
Can face damnation?

Or's my punishment
To spend eternity in
Search of you. Perhaps,

Though, I am simply
Afraid of death. Perhaps I
Don't have your brav'ry.

Give me strength, lady!
There is that chill again. It
Must be death's fingers,

For Apollo is
Awake. He rides high and has
Already, in scorn,

Burned away morning's
Tears of dew and let the stench
Of death ride upon

The sea breeze. Still, I
Shiver. Let me share your rug,
My love, share the warmth.

And when they find our
Bodies, they will find us, hand
In hand, heart to heart.

Hands do not fail me!
Guide the steel true!

He stabs himself.

Passes. So he dies.

Give me your hand, my
Lady, while I still see. Let
Me kiss your fingers.

Had we but met in
Another time, dear lover,
In another place.

> *AJAX dies.*
>
> *Moments later, ODYSSEUS
> wanders in. He is still a little
> drunk. He looks around for
> AJAX, but cannot see him.
> He takes in the scene of ovine
> carnage.*

ODYSSEUS

Well, Ajax. It looks
As if you had about as
Much fun as we did.

What did these poor sheep
Ever do to you? It does
Not matter. They must

Surely have deserved
It. Anyway, I am pooped.
Have not done that in

A while. Remember
That small town near Hisarlik?
Well, I don't either.

Who does? Who will? We're
At Troy! One of the greatest
Of cities, jewel of

An empire, beacon
Of hope and culture! Who cares
'Bout some hamlet in

Anatolia?
But you'll remember those twins.
The ones we found in

The cellar. Had to
Wrap them in horseflesh to sneak
Them by the men. Fools.

But they were worth it.
Except for the smell. I have
Not had such fun since

That night. Briseis,
Though! I wish that you had joined
Us. Oh, that wacky

Nestor. I'm afraid
He was gnawing on her. That
Is, by the third or

Fourth time I went in,
There were some pieces missing.
Like pounding on a

Dead pig, after a
While. But what are you going
To do? Is there wine?

He drinks from a flask.

Gods! This swill.

He finds another flask and
drinks from it.

Better.
So. Mutton tonight? Ha, ha!
Anyhoo, I stopped

By to make sure there
Were no hard feelings. After,
Well, last night, you know.

I suppose she is
Around someplace. Briseis,
I mean. Unless, of

Course, Nestor ate her.
Strange man. You know what I mean.
Ajax! Ajax! Where

Is he? Not around.
Just Odysseus alone,
With all these dead sheep.

BRISEIS, covered, stirs and moans.

What's that? Who is that?
A spy! A spy! Help! Help! Ho!
Then die! Trojan swine!

He hacks BRISEIS to pieces.

Let's take a look at
What brave fool did sneak in here
Disguised as a lamb.

He reveals BRISEIS but not AJAX.

Oh. It's you. I thought
Perhaps I'd slain a hero,
But I killed a whore.

It wasn't you. It
Wasn't personal. I had
To trick Ajax. When

Our host assembled
To sail on Troy, I did not
Wish to come here. It

Was a pointless war.
I didn't trust my wife. I'd
Rather not die here.

So, I feigned madness.
I hitched my finest horses
To a common plough

And charged up and down
My fields. In retrospect, I'm
Not sure how that act

Demonstrated that
I was mad. But it seemed like
A plan at the time.

It was Ajax who
Outsmarted me. Guessing that
My madness was false,

He placed my infant
Son, my Telemachus, in
Chariot's path. I

Had to swerve. Ajax
Bested me. I'm the clever
One. But fool Ajax,

Ajax the lummox,
Outsmarted Odysseus?
Couldn't let that go.

Could not let Ajax
Beat vulpine Odysseus.
Oh, no. I could not.

It may seem petty
To you. But it is not as
If I could beat him

At feats of strength. Look
At me. I'm no warrior.
I'm not. To my shame.

I'm the clever one!
Could I permit the balance
To lean t'wards Ajax?

I had no choice, you
See. That you happened to be
The object of our

Competition? Luck?
Circumstance? Happenstance? Fate?
P'rhaps our good fortune.

I thought you'd survive.
How was I to know Nestor
Would be so...hungry?

So, have you seen him?
Would you tell me if you could?
If you were living?

You Trojans are a
Tricky lot. You sneaked in here,
Disguised as a sheep.

What was your plan? What
Are you hiding from me? Talk.
I can make you talk.

You know where Ajax
Is. You know. Why must you be
So difficult? Why?

Do I need to call
Nestor again? He'll come. He
Won't care that you're dead.

I'm fighting with a
Dead Trojan. A dead woman.
This war's been too long.

I am tired of this.

> *He sits on AJAX.*

Ajax! Come on out! Ajax!
We'll clean up this mess.

We'll make it all right!
This is one huge sheep! We'll be
Eating it for weeks.

This is—

                    (Realizing)
        Oh, my. Gods!

> *He reveals AJAX's body.*

Ajax! Dear friend! Speak to me!
Oh, what have you done?

It was not supposed
To end like this. You and I
Were supposed to live.

Speak to me. Is there
Yet a spark? Ajax! Friend! Live!
There's nor spark nor air

Great Ajax is slain.
No Trojan sword nor dart could
Bring this hero down.

Only a gentle
Smile and dancing eyes could be
His bane. Had I known

How much this trollop
Meant to you, I never would
Have stolen her. Friend,

Believe me, we were
Supposed to live. I had it
Planned. Let Troy fall. Let

Heroes die and Greeks
Rot on this wasted dirt. We
Would make it. We'd live.

And together we
Would sail from these forsaken
Shores. Together we

Would make it to our
Homes. We could grow old, and sit,
Together, by our

Fires, on our thrones, and
Tell our wives, our children, our
Descendants such tales

Of heroism,
Of glory days and our parts
In them. What stories

We could have told them,
Dear friend, and we would have been
Remembered. We'd be

Likened to the gods.
We'd be the principals of
This great conflict and

Central to councils
And stratagems. The poets
Would compose epics

About us, for we
Would be the only ones left
To pay for them. How

Could you do this? How
Could you die and leave me all
Alone? I would have

Given you the girl,
The damnéd girl. Oh, Ajax,
You've had the last laugh,

For you…have tricked…me.
You have cheated. Cheated me
Of my companion,

Cheated me of my
Friend. The lesson is dear, friend,
But I have learned it.

We will never laugh
About this trick. E'en clever
Odysseus can't

Turn back death once it
Has crossed the threshold. Even
I can't bring you back.

Is it dark there? Do
Your dead sheep nuzzle you? Does
Briseis embrace

You? Are you alone?
What adventure is this, now?
Without companion?

Without a friend to
Guide you past whatever traps
And obstacles you

Find. I pray she's there.
I pray they are there, Ajax.
For you. For Ajax.

Who's to stay with me?
Odysseus must face his
Future alone. No

One to give him strength.
No one to love, for there is
No love so strong as

That between two great
Men, warriors, kings, equals.
Romantic love's pale.

It can be given,
Taken from a slave. Bought, sold
On a street corner.

Is that love? Even
Animals have sex. Women
Mewl and simper, pout

Their lips and hiss like
Lust-driven serpents that sting
And suck 'way our strength.

They can feign love. They
Can pretend excitement. They
Moan and sigh! They groan!

While deep inside they
Loathe us for the fools that we
Make ourselves for them.

Take the damned woman!
Take her. Use her. Let her dry
Up, age, grow fat, grow

Ugly, then cast her
Aside like offal, garbage.
That's not.... That's not love.

Love's confronting storms
Together, being showered
With an enemy's

Guts and blood. Love is
Crawling through the desert, no
Water for days, the

Heat clawing at your
Brain. Love is braving a swarm
Of arrows as you

Share your last crust, is
Standing back to back before
The full fury of

A great empire, is
Coughing through the smoke and stench
Of a sacked city,

Enjoying a slave
Girls' tears, the pleas of the lost.
That is what love is.

Love is not dancing
Barefoot amidst the flowers,
Singing like a bird,

Or children laughing.
Oh, no. Love is facing life
And death together.

Now I must face life
Alone. Whatever journey
The Fates have planned for

Me I face alone.
Whatever punishments are
Prepared for me in

Hell I must now face
Alone. Will you tarry? Will
You wait for me? Dear

Ajax, I am done
With tricks and games for they have
Brought me naught but pain.

I shall turn my thoughts
To plots and stratagems. I
Will have vengeance on

Troy for losing you.
I would happily have left,
Have abandoned this

Pointless war. The death
Of Achilles, the virtue
Of Helen are naught

To me. However,
The fall of Ajax means much.
Dear Briseis, your

People can thank you
For their fate. I shall not rest
Until your home lies

In ruin. The smoke
Of her host a great cloud that
Blocks out the sun's rays,

Her women abused,
Enslaved, her children tossed from
High cliffs into the

Raging seas, her fields
Salted. Odysseus is
Master of his own

Life now, teller of
His own story. Sing muses,
Of this man who will

Face down the very
Gods and make his own fate. Let
Children cry and let

Women shudder at
My epic. Let it fill all
With pity and fear.

Oh, Ajax. I will
Search throughout the world for a
Road to Hades. P'rhaps

There I will find you.
Will you still speak to me, then?
Will you still love me?

NESTOR and CHORUS OF SOLDIERS
(Singing offstage)

Fa la la, fa la la, derry derry derry doh,
For Nestor's cock is here!

Fa la la, fa la la, derry derry derry doh,
For Nestor's cock is here!

ODYSSEUS

Listen to the fools.
Let them have their amusement.
In but a moment,

I will leave this place.
I shall take my place in the
Tents of the mighty.

I can't avoid this
Pointless war, did start it.
But I can end it.

ODYSSEUS exits.

CURTAIN

MUSIC

Nestor's Song

Part 1 - Nestor

Edward Eaton

Edward Eaton

Pray to your gods and hide your daugh - ters,

For Nes-tor's cock is here to-night Fa la la Fa la la

Der-ry der-ry der-ry doh For Nes - tor's cock is here.

A - pol - lo, hang your head in shame O While your Mu - ses

spread their shape - ly legs Fa la la Fa la la

Der-ry der-ry der-ry doh For Nes - tor's cock is here.

Poor young Bri - se - is screams and fights so, My migh - ty thrust does shut her up   Fa   la la   Fa la la

Der - ry   der - ry der - ry   doh   For   Nes - tor's cock   is   here.

Stand   all   you Greeks   and cheer for   Nes - tor.   Look on in en -

vy   at   his might   Fa   la la   Fa la la   Der-ry   der-ry der-ry

doh   For   Nes - tor's   cock   is   here.

Nestor's Song

Edward Eaton

Refrain

Edward Eaton

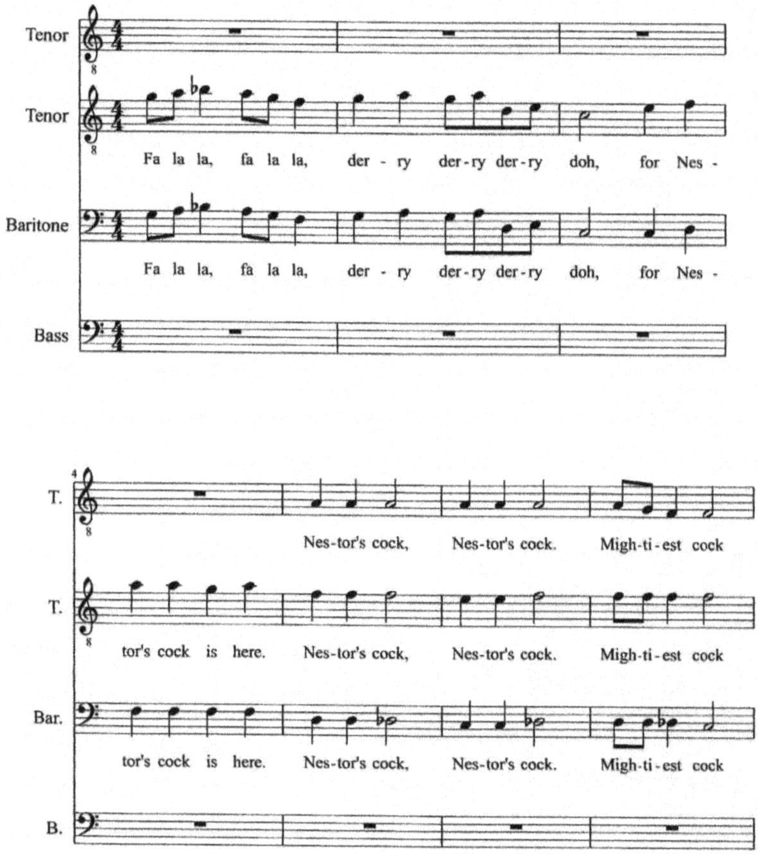

T. in Greece. Tro-jans fear. Wo-men shriek.

T. in Greece. Tro-jans fear. Wo-men shriek.

Bar. in Greece. Tro-jans fear. Wo-men shriek.

B. Tro-Jans fear. Wo-men shriek.

T. Con-quer-or of the we - ee - ak!

T. Con-quer-er of the we - ee - ak!

Bar. Con-quer-or of the we - ee - ak

B. The We - ak!

Nestor's Song

Part 2 - Odysseus' Part

Edward Eaton

Edward Eaton

Nes - tor was such an an - cient he - ro No one thought the

thing would work oh Fa la la, fa la la Der ry der ry der - ry

doh For Nes - tor's cock is here. He rose to - night to the o - cca - sion,

He took Bri - se - is, first in line Fa la la Fa la la

Der ry der ry der ry doh For Nes - tor's cock is here.

Screams we have heard and so have wondered, What What has this an -

cient Nes - tor done? Fa la la, fa la la Der ry der ry der ry

doh For Nes tor's cock is here. Bruised and bat - terred is fair Bri - se - is

Tes - ti - mo - ny to Nes - tor's might Fa la la Fa la la

Der - ry der - ry der - ry doh For Nes - tor's cock is here.

Nestor's Song

Edward Eaton

Refrain

Edward Eaton

Fa la la, fa la la, der - ry der - ry der - ry doh, for Nes -

Fa la la, fa la la, der - ry der - ry der - ry doh, for Nes -

Nes-tor's cock, Nes-tor's cock. Migh-ti - est cock

tor's cock is here. Nes-tor's cock, Nes-tor's cock. Migh-ti - est cock

tor's cock is here. Nes-tor's cock, Nes-tor's cock. Migh-ti - est cock

T. in Greece. Tro-jans fear. Wo-men shriek.

T. in Greece. Tro-jans fear. Wo-men shriek.

Bar. in Greece. Tro-jans fear. Wo-men shriek.

B. Tro-Jans fear. Wo-men shriek.

T. Con-quer-or of the we - ee - ak!

T. Con-quer-er of the we - ee - ak!

Bar. Con-quer-or of the we - ee - ak

B. The We - ak!

Nestor's Song

Part 3 - Chorus of Soldiers' Part

Edward Eaton

Edward Eaton

Voice: Nes-tor's a king we want to fol-low. He'll give us lots of lus-ty whores

Vo.: Fa la la, fa la la, Der ry der ry der-ry doh. For Nes-

Vo.: tor's cock is here. He breaks his fing-ers as he beats them,

Vo.: Ma-king it ea-si-er for us Fa la la Fa la la Der ry der ry der ry

Vo.: doh. For Nes-tor's cock is here. Though Nes-tor must be o-ver eight-y

Vo.: He rapes like he's a lad of twen-ty. Fa la la, fa la la

Vo.: Der ry der ry der ry doh For Nes tor's cock is here. When I grow old,

Vo.: I want to be like The Nes-tor we have seen to-night

Vo.: Fa la la Fa la la Der-ry der-ry der-ry doh For Nes-tor's cock is here.

Nestor's Song

Edward Eaton

Refrain

Edward Eaton

Tenor

Tenor
Fa la la, fa la la, der - ry der - ry der - ry doh, for Nes -

Baritone
Fa la la, fa la la, der - ry der - ry der - ry doh, for Nes -

Bass

T.
Nes - tor's cock, Nes - tor's cock. Migh - ti - est cock

T.
tor's cock is here. Nes - tor's cock, Nes - tor's cock. Migh - ti - est cock

Bar.
tor's cock is here. Nes - tor's cock, Nes - tor's cock. Migh - ti - est cock

B.

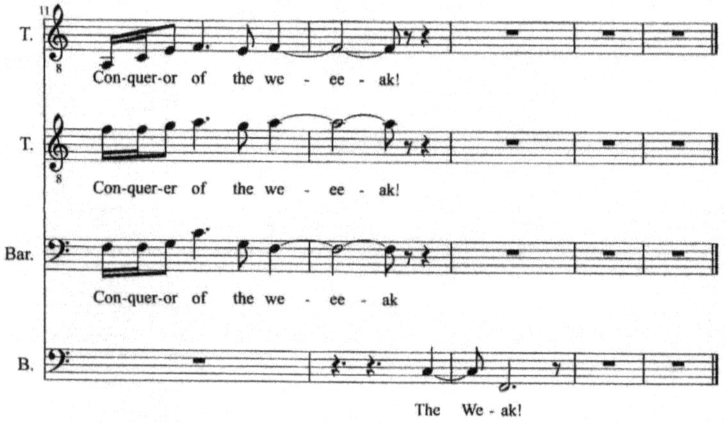

Nestor's Song

Edward Eaton

Fa la las

Edward Eaton

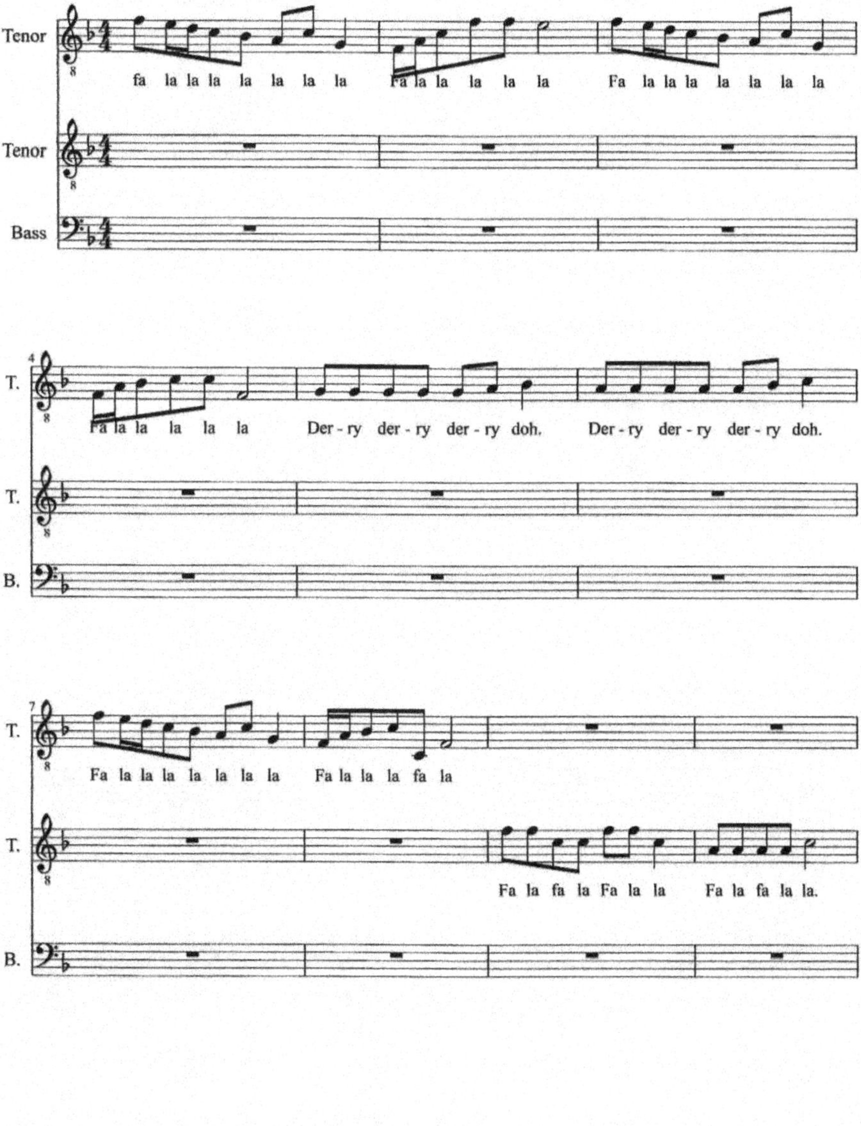

11
T.
T.
Fa la fa la fa la la, Fa la fa la la. Der - ry der - ry der - ry doh,
B.
14
T.
T.
Der-ry der-ry der-ry doh. Fa la fa la fa la la, Fal la la fa la.
B.
Der - ry der - ry
18
T.
T.
B.
der-ry doh, der-ry der-ry der-ry doh. Fa la fa la, fa la fa la. Der-ry der-ry

24
T.
fa la la la la la la la Fa la la la la la
T.
Fa la fa la Fa la la Fa la fa la la.
B.
der - ry doh! Der - ry der - ry der - ry doh,
28
T.
Fa la la la la la la la Fa la la la la la Der-ry der-ry der-ry doh.
T.
Fa la fa la fa la la, Fa la fa la la. Der-ry der-ry der-ry doh,
B.
der - ry der - ry der - ry doh. Fa la fa la,
31
T.
Der-ry der-ry der-ry doh. Fa la la la la la la la Fa la la la fa la
T.
Der-ry der-ry der-ry doh. Fa la fa la fa la la, Fal la la fa la.
B.
fa la fa la. Der - ry der - ry der - ry doh!

Nestor's Song
Finale

Edward Eaton

Edward Eaton

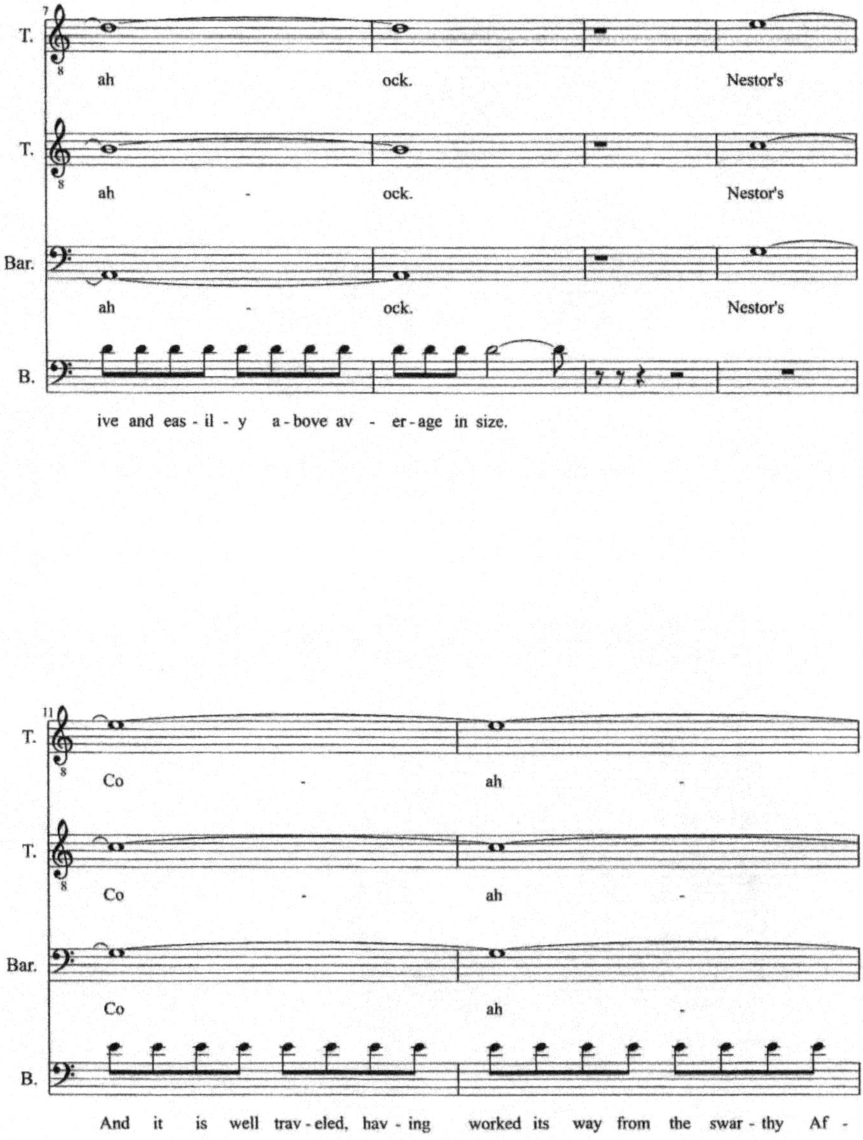
7
T.
ah ock. Nestor's
T.
ah - ock. Nestor's
Bar.
ah - ock. Nestor's
B.
ive and eas - il - y a - bove av - er - age in size.
11
T.
Co - ah -
T.
Co - ah -
Bar.
Co ah -
B.
And it is well trav - eled, hav - ing worked its way from the swar - thy Af -

13
T.
ah - ck! - Nestor's
T.
ah - ock! - Nestor's
Bar.
ah - ock! - Nestor's
B.
ric jun - gles to the fri - gid Nor - dic Seas.

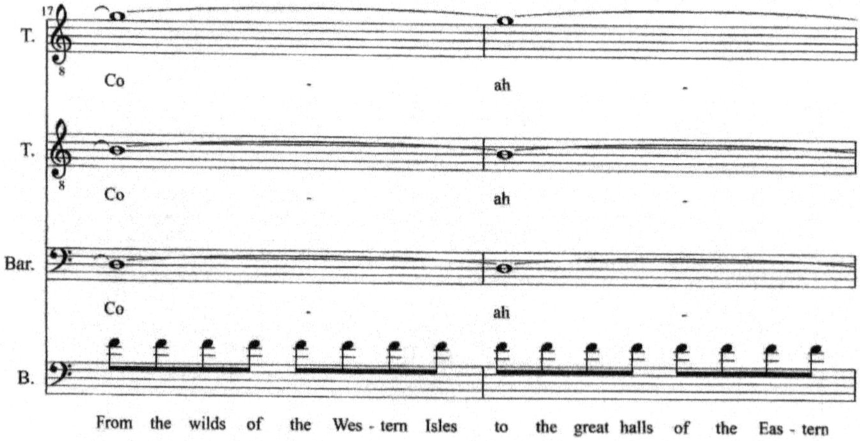
17
T.
Co - ah -
T.
Co - ah -
Bar.
Co - ah -
B.
From the wilds of the Wes - tern Isles to the great halls of the Eas - tern

T. ock! Nestor's Co -

T. ock! Nestor's Co -

Bar. ock! Nestor's Co -

B. Em-pires, it is feared. It is al - ways will - ing, though gi -

T. ah - ah - ock!

T. ah - ah - ock!

Bar. ah - ah - ock!

B. ven that Nes - tor is ov - ver eight - y it might not al - ways be ab - ble.

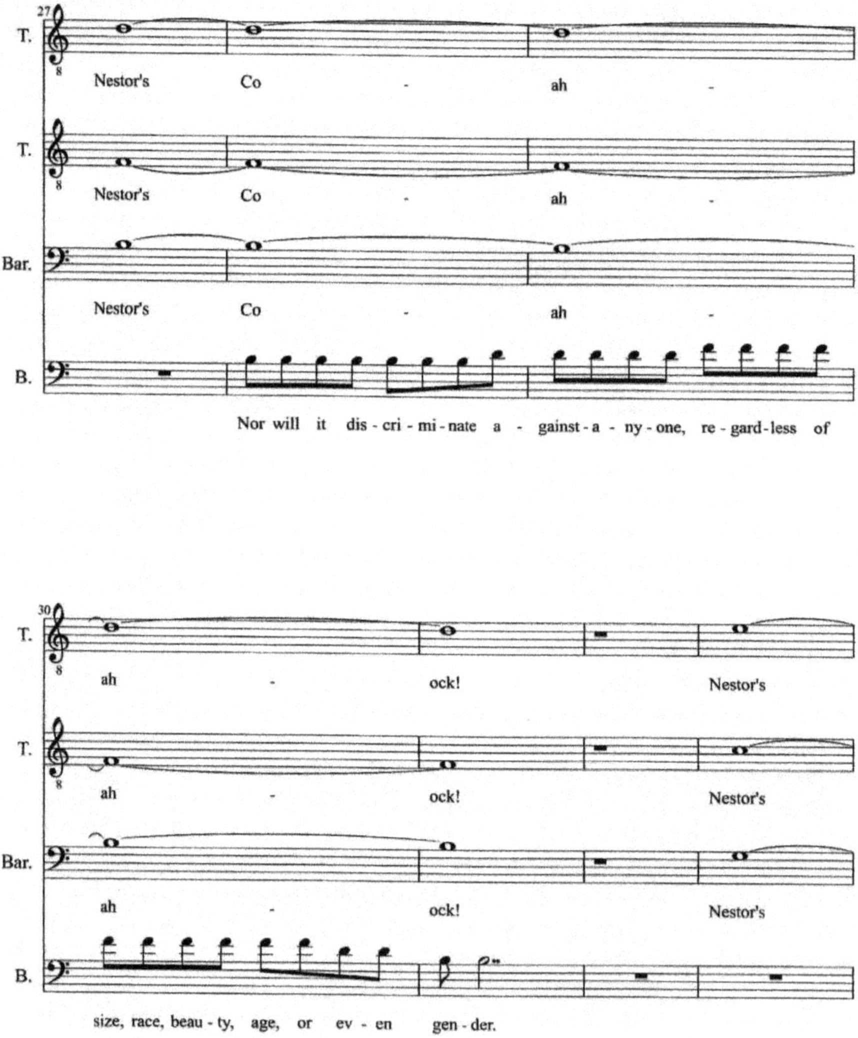
27
T.
Nestor's Co - ah -
T.
Nestor's Co - ah -
Bar.
Nestor's Co - ah -
B.
Nor will it dis - cri - mi - nate a - gainst - a - ny - one, re - gard - less of
30
T.
ah - ock! Nestor's
T.
ah - ock! Nestor's
Bar.
ah - ock! Nestor's
B.
size, race, beau - ty, age, or ev - en gen - der.

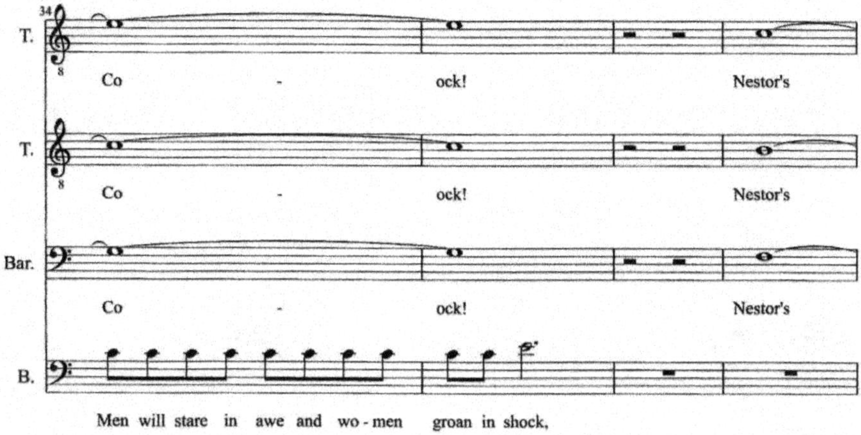
34
T.
Co - ock! Nestor's
T.
Co - ock! Nestor's
Bar.
Co - ock! Nestor's
B.
Men will stare in awe and wo - men groan in shock,

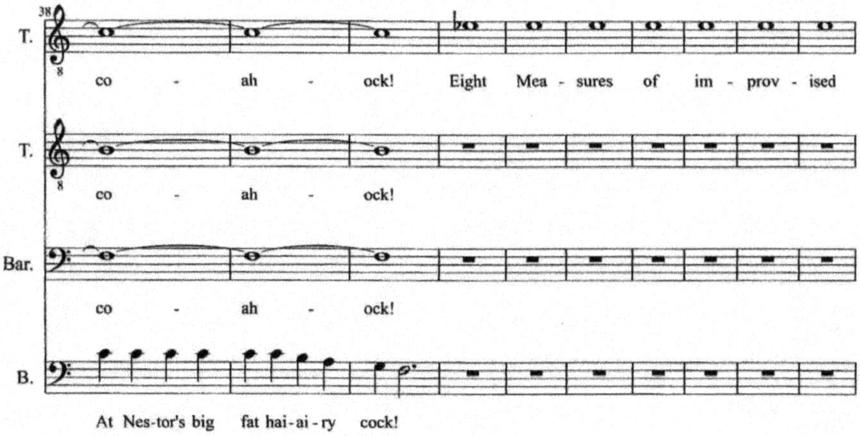
38
T.
co - ah - ock! Eight Mea - sures of im - prov - ised
T.
co - ah - ock!
Bar.
co - ah - ock!
B.
At Nes-tor's big fat hai-ai-ry cock!

48
T.
scat Nes - tor's Co - ock!
T.
Nes - tor's co - ock!
Bar.
Nes - tor's co - ock!
B.
Nes - tor's co - ock!

About the Author

EDWARD Eaton has studied and taught at many schools in the States, China, Israel, Oman, and France. He holds a PhD in Theatre History and Literature and has worked extensively as a theatre director and fight choreographer. As a writer, he has been a newspaper columnist, a theatre critic, and has published and presented many scholarly papers.

He is the author of the award-winning *Rosi's Doors* young adult series, which includes the following titles: Rosi's Castle, Rosi's Time, and Rosi's Company. Drama publications include Elizabeth Bathory, Giants Fall, Hector and Achilles, and Orpheus and Eurydice. Other publications include the epic verse Toh's Saga.

In addition to his academic and creative pursuits, he is an avid SCUBA diver and skier. He currently lives and works in Boston, Massachusetts, with his wife Silviya and his son Christopher.

Visit the author's website at:: www.edwardeaton.com.

* * * * *

www.ingramcontent.com/pod-product-compliance
Lightning Source LLC
LaVergne TN
LVHW011321080426
835513LV00006B/153